# The Coolest Guys on Ice

# The Coolest Guys on Ice

*by Jeff Z. Klein and Karl-Eric Reif*

*Foreword by Pat LaFontaine*

Turner Publishing, Inc.
Atlanta

Library of Congress Cataloging-in-Publication Data

Klein, Jeff Z.
The coolest guys on ice/by Jeff Z. Klein and Karl-Eric Reif.-1st ed.
p.      cm.
ISBN 1-57036-362-5 (alk. paper)
1. Hockey players-Biography. I. Reif, Karl-Eric. II. Title.
GV848.5.A1K54  1996
796.964'092273-dc20
[B]        96-21376
CIP

ISBN: 1-57036-362-5

PUBLISHED BY TURNER PUBLISHING, INC.

A SUBSIDIARY OF TURNER BROADCASTING SYSTEM, INC.

1050 TECHWOOD DRIVE, N. W.

ATLANTA, GA 30318

IN COOPERATION WITH NHL ENTERPRISES, INC.

1251 AVENUE OF THE AMERICAS

NEW YORK, NY 10020-1198

DISTRIBUTED BY ANDREWS AND MCMEEL

A UNIVERSAL PRESS SYNDICATE COMPANY

4900 MAIN STREET

KANSAS CITY, MO 64112

FIRST EDITION 10 9 8 7 6 5 4 3 2 1

PRINTED IN THE U. S. A.

# Contents

# Introduction

The U.S. hockey team's "Miracle on Ice" at the 1980 Winter Olympics was an inspiration for countless hockey fans—including me, as well as many other young American players. I'll never forget the date of that big victory over the Soviets: it was February 22—my fifteenth birthday.

At game's end, the emotion and enthusiasm of Mike Eruzione, Jim Craig, and the rest of the U.S. Olympians was outright contagious. It stirred up a lot of patriotic fervor, too, but I didn't care too much about that. It was just a terrific time to be playing hockey in America, and it helped one teenage hockey player, who before then only hoped to earn a college scholarship, dream about one day playing in the Olympics against the best the world had to offer.

As I write this and prepare to play in the first World Cup of Hockey tournament, I'm reminded of how global the sport has become since 1980. When I was growing up, North Americans would hear about players from Europe and Russia only during the Olympics and the Canada Cup. Today, foreign-born players are a fixture of the sport in the U.S. and Canada, even in junior hockey. With so many of the best players from around the world now playing in North America in the National Hockey League, the fans have come to know and appreciate the international players on all of the NHL teams. Seeing them compete for their own countries will make a tournament like the World Cup a very special event.

My first game against players from outside North America came at the start of the U.S. team's 58-game warm-up tour for the 1984 Winter Olympics. We were up against a Soviet B team in Anchorage, Alaska. From the start, the game had a different feeling than any I'd ever played. Wearing the red, white, and blue, and playing against Russians, I was as far away from my Michigan home as I could get and still be on American soil. Right away, I was amazed by the Soviet players' quickness, the level of their skills, their stickhandling, and even just the way they all played their system so well. They'd make three or four precise passes, and all of a sudden there'd be a breakaway and we'd all be chasing them.

Despite the patriotism the Olympics always produces, often in excess, I never have anything but respect for the opposing teams. I remember sitting in the crowd in Sarajevo and spotting one of the Russian players I'd competed against a year or so earlier in Alaska. He recognized me immediately and waved from the ice, even with all that was on the line for him. Player to player, there never were many national boundaries.

Even before I made it to the Olympics, it was obvious that hockey was becoming more international. In the 1972 Summit Series, the first time NHL stars faced off against serious foreign competition, the Soviets spanked Team Canada 7-3 right in the Montreal Forum, winning two of the first four games decisively. Team Canada rallied to take the series with three consecutive one-goal wins in Moscow, but the world was on notice: North America had no monopoly on hockey talent.

My favorite NHL players when I was growing up were Guy Lafleur of the Montreal Canadiens and the Buffalo Sabres' Gilbert Perreault. But there were other great skaters with great skills that I admired, like the Swedish stars Borje Salming and Kent Nilsson. They called Nilsson "the magic man." Guys I've played with talked about how Nilsson would bet teammates at practice that he could hit the crossbar four out of five times in a row from the red line. He usually won.

By the time I made it to the NHL in 1984, European players were no longer a novelty simply because of their nationality. The New York Rangers' Finnish defenseman Reijo Ruotsaleinen was one player who made a big impression on me; Tomas Jonsson and Stefan Persson, both Swedes, were two of our best defensemen on the Islanders. Off the ice, I learned some Finnish from fellow Islander Mikko Makela and a little Czech from another teammate, David Volek. Now I'm with the Sabres, and one of our goaltenders, Dominik Hasek, is Czech; the other, Andrei Trefilov, is Russian.

I feel fortunate to have joined the league when I did. Anyone who's played in the NHL since the 1980s has really seen change, with the influx of international players as well as other influences. When I started playing, no one would've believed that the league's all-time record for regular-season wins would be posted by a team from Detroit with a core of Russia's best players, as happened this past season. Or that there'd be two teams in Florida, of all places, and one in Anaheim called the "Mighty Ducks."

When you watch the NHL today, you witness an array of skills and styles perfected in rinks all around the world. It's a much quicker game, with a higher skill level, than it was when I started, when maybe a few guys on every team were either really big or could really skate. Now every team has huge guys who can motor as well as shoot.

Playing in the 1984 Olympics was the fulfillment of a dream for me. Now, more than sixteen years after first beginning to hope for a chance to compete in the Olympics, I'm fulfilling another dream by being able to play in the World Cup. An international tournament featuring all of the world's best professionals is truly a landmark event. For all the speed and skill European players have brought to the game, to my mind the greatest effect their presence has had on the NHL is to promote tolerance. Fans are still fiercely loyal, and players still have the competitive fire inside. But society has grown. People understand that there's great hockey talent all over the world. The world's best hockey talent gathered together to play the world's best hockey—what more could any fan ask for? Playing at that level in a tournament that will be watched around the world is what this year's crop of fifteen-year-old hockey players will be dreaming about tomorrow.

PAT LaFONTAINE
AMHERST, NEW YORK
JULY, 1996

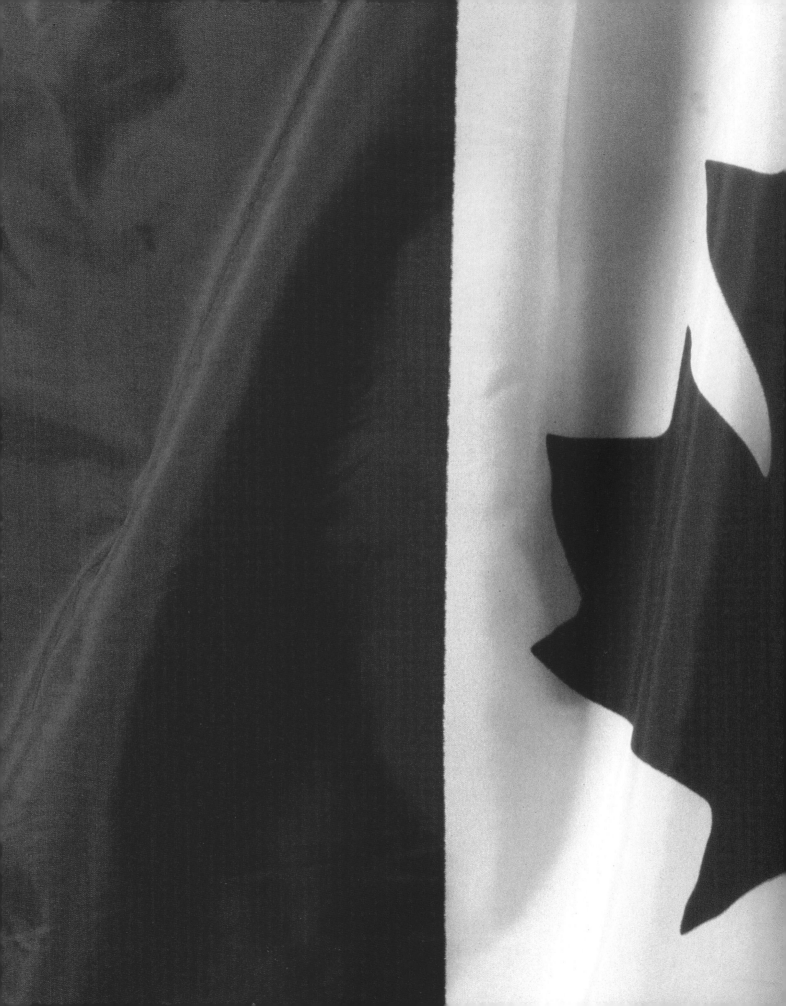

# Canada

Think of Canada, and you think of hockey. Canadians may protest that there's much more to their country than that, but the objection is tempered by their love for a game profoundly rooted in their national identity. After a century and a quarter in which both the sport and the nation were born and grew to maturity, hockey has become so fundamental to being Canadian that the discourse surrounding the game has become a kind of shorthand, a means to connect points in a shared knowledge and experience.

The Canadian identity is wound inextricably with the visceral experience of living with hockey on a day-to-day basis. Someone in your family plays the game at some level, your team is the topic of conversation at school or at work, Saturdays are "Hockey Night in Canada." Hockey players aren't just celebrities but touchstones of a common experience: someone looks like that player, someone works as hard as another player, someone you know grew up next door to yet another.

Mention a player's name, and it's more than just a face or a sweater or a few stats that come to mind. He represents something larger—success, failure, enthusiasm, apathy, bravery, cowardice, pride, shame, artistry, clumsiness, an abundance of talent or an absence of it—and the moments in time, the moments on the ice, when he embodied those things. Cite a big game, using no more than the opponents and the season, and it too is richly allusive, of a moment of fulfillment or frustration, of glory or despair.

From its roots in Indian games played on frozen ponds and in European ball-and-stick games, to its birth in the Kingston or Montreal or Halifax of the 1870s as a formal sport with official rules, hockey has always been the Canadian game. From Lord Stanley's purchase of a small silver bowl, to players like One-Eyed Frank McGee, Newsy Lalonde, and Cyclone Taylor to Bad Joe Hall, Georges Vezina, and Howie Morenz, hockey cemented together a still-young nation, linking a vast winter landscape as surely as the railroads and the telegraph. From King Clancy, Charlie Conacher, and Eddie Shore to Rocket Richard, Gordie Howe, and Jacques Plante, from Bobby Hull, Bobby Orr, and Guy Lafleur to Wayne Gretzky, Mark Messier, and Mario Lemieux, Canada and hockey are synonymous. Whether in the Patrick brothers' establishment of a Pacific Coast league, symbolizing the urbanization of the remote Far West, or in French Canada's struggles with self-identity and nationhood, as bookended by the Richard Riot and L'affaire Lindros, or in the rare mass expressions of Canadian patriotism ignited by the '72 series and more recent Canada Cup and Olympic showdowns, the story of hockey is the story of Canada.

With a legacy as rich as this, who, then, could blame Canadians for thinking hockey was their game and theirs alone? Canada was the only country that lived and breathed hockey, the only one in which it was talked about year round. But other countries had begun to learn it, applying their own cultural motifs to it, beginning to excel at it, slowly building their own modest traditions.

In 1972, Canada learned to its utter amazement and horror that this was so. They needed Paul Henderson's last-minute goal to beat the Soviet Union, a country that they had dismissed as less than mere pretenders. Canada would never be the same.

But even though Canada had learned it was no longer the only country capable of playing hockey well, it still remained on top. They beat the rest of the world's best in four out of five Canada Cup tournaments. And although the best Soviet teams could now match Canada's all-stars, the best players were still Canadian, and Canada was still where the best from around the world wanted to go to prove their mettle.

Hockey is no longer Canada's alone. More than a third of NHL players are American, European, or from the old Soviet Union, and the number grows, NHL expansion franchises go to American Sun Belt cities, and the economics of sports even force teams in smaller Canadian cities to move to the United States. Understandably, Canadians feel they're being robbed of their sporting heritage. But Canada can take pride in hockey as its gift to the world, that its great invention is now as loved across the planet's northern nations as it is in its birthplace. And it is growing still, into the land of palm trees and who knows where else next?...

# Ray Bourque

TWENTY YEARS AGO, IF YOU'D ASKED A PANEL OF HOCKEY EXPERTS TO NAME THE TWO BEST DEFENSEMEN ever to play the game, chances are they'd have answered Bobby Orr—unquestionably the greatest rearguard in history—and '20s and '30s legend Eddie Shore. It just so happens that even though their careers were separated by some 40 years, they were both Boston Bruins. 🏒 If you were to ask that same question today, the answer would still be Orr, and, probably, some kind of toss up between Shore and another Bruin, the greatest blueliner of our generation—Ray Bourque. 🏒 The only player in NHL history to be honored as a First or Second Team All-Star in every single season he's played (an incredible 17-year string), Ray Bourque has won the Norris Trophy as the league's outstanding defenseman five times. Only Orr and Montreal immortal Doug Harvey were honored more often. Bourque's consistently sterling defensive play is almost lost in the glare of his relentless offensive production. Since entering the NHL in 1979, when he set a record for rookie defensemen with 65 points and won the Calder Trophy, Bourque has scored 20 or more goals nine times, five times led his team in scoring, and generated better than a point a game in 15 of his 17 seasons, amassing 343 goals, 970 assists, and 1,313 points through 1995-96. He stands just behind Paul Coffey, and head and shoulders above every other blueliner, in every major career scoring category. 🏒 "Numbers aren't everything," states the typically modest Bourque. "You've got to look at wins and losses as well. That's what I look at, not my numbers. They're fine, and things are going well for me, but all those numbers are thrown out if you don't make the playoffs, or don't get somewhere in the playoffs. That's what it's all about. That's why we play." 🏒 And while that ultimate goal—the Stanley Cup—has so far sadly eluded Bourque, just as it eluded Dionne, Perreault, Ratelle, Gadsby, Salming, Howell, and others throughout lengthy Hall of Fame careers, he remains in the hunt. Bourque has almost single-handedly carried the Bruins to the Cup Final twice, and stands as the primary reason why teams from Beantown have continued their remarkable skein of 29 consecutive post-season appearances. 🏒 "To me," says Wayne Gretzky, "the reason why Boston year in and year out is consistently near the top is obviously because of him. I don't know if there's any defenseman in hockey who's as complete a player as he is. For that matter, I don't know if there's another player in the game who's as complete as he is." 🏒 Gretzky speaks for almost everyone; no player in hockey is more respected by teammates,

*AMAZING GRACE-Boston's Ray Bourque outskates two Rangers to the puck.*

opponents, and fans than Bourque.

"His work ethic is incredible," says Steve Kasper, a former teammate and now the ninth head coach in Bourque's Bruin career. "It's amazing to watch. He has that capability to inspire the whole team."

"Whatever pace Ray wants the game at, that's the pace the game is played at," observes another former teammate, Peter McNab.

"Gretzky does it, Lemieux does it—only those guys you'll remember in your all-dream team."

Wayne Cashman, whose 17-year Bruin career was winding down just as Bourque's was beginning, says simply, "There's Ray Bourque and then whoever else had a good year. That's how it's been for fifteen years."

Game after game, Bourque logs more minutes on the ice than anyone else in the NHL. Yet his tremendous conditioning and prodigious skills—his muscular skating and great balance, his uncannily accurate shooting and passing, his superb anticipation, instincts, and timing—still don't fully account for his unflagging excellence in regular-season, postseason, and international play.

Another former Bruin, Gord Kluzak, points to Bourque's heart. "Ray is such a proud and passionate guy. He cares so much. That's what allowed him to do what he's done—his love for the game, his passion for the game, and being very competitive." Those qualities make Bourque the natural choice to be the Bruins' captain, a post he has held since 1988.

The eighth choice overall in the '79 draft after a fabulous career in the Quebec junior league, Bourque is a clean player; he has never taken more than 96 penalty minutes in a single season. Yet for all his astounding talent, for all the acclaim and respect, Bourque, a private and quiet man, has made the startling admission that he is really driven by fear. "I know no one has ever played a perfect game," he told the *Boston Globe.* "But, shift after shift, I'm afraid of doing something wrong—I'm afraid to make a mistake, afraid to be embarrassed out there, afraid that I won't get the job done. Why? I don't know. It's just always been with me, ever since I was a little kid. I've just got it, and without it, I wouldn't be anywhere near the player I am."

The thought of playing with Bourque "sends chills up and down my spine," said Bruins rookie defenseman Kyle McLaren at the start of the 1995-96 campaign. "I like listening to

I don't know if there's any defenseman in hockey who's as complete a player as he is.

him, because he knows his stuff. It's just unreal what he can teach me. When he retires, I'd like to take his mind, exchange brains—yeah, that's it, I'd like to use his brain the rest of my career."

"It's funny," says Bourque, whose career stretches from the era of such Bruin greats as Rick Middleton, Brad Park, and Terry O'Reilly to the recent heyday of Cam Neely and Adam Oates. "I know I've played a kids' game for 17 years and I'm 35 years old, but that's not the way it feels. I look around the dressing room and see kids like Kyle, and I don't say, 'Gee, I'm 35.' I feel like I'm in my mid-20s, like I'm a big part of it, and I want to keep playing as long as I can keep performing well and contribute on defense. I don't want to fade out. I dread the time I won't be able to play the way I want."

In 1995-96, Bourque added another 20-goal season to his long list of achievements, an 82-point effort in which he again led the team in plus/minus by a whopping margin. He also scored the winning goal late in the midseason All-Star Game in Boston, sparking a long, raucous outpouring of affection from the home-town fans. At 35, he simply shows no sign of slowing down.

"I'm still doing something I love," he says. "It's great getting up in the morning knowing that you're going to work and you're doing what you want to be doing."

For hockey fans, it's great getting to the rink whenever Ray Bourque's in town, knowing that you're going to see one of the very best ever to play the game.

# Wayne Gretzky

WAYNE GRETZKY, THE GREATEST PLAYER IN THE HISTORY OF HOCKEY, HAS LINED THE FABULOUS HIGHWAY of his career with one towering achievement after another. From his Ontario childhood, when his miraculous talent already received national attention; though his first pro season, when he scored 110 points for Indianapolis and Edmonton of the WHA; through his rookie year in the NHL, when he scored 51 goals, led the league in assists, tied for the league lead in points, and won the Hart Trophy as the NHL's most valuable player, all while still a teenager; through eight more years in Edmonton, in which he smashed nearly every NHL single-season and play-off scoring record and then smashed his own records again and again, led the league in scoring by ever-increasing margins for seven consecutive years, and led the Oilers to four Stanley Cups; through starring roles in international challenge tournaments; through his earth-shattering trade in 1988 to the Los Angeles Kings; through seven and a half seasons in L.A. in which he won three more NHL scoring titles, breathed life into the franchise, and helped to at last make hockey a national sport throughout the U.S. 🏒 A February 1996 trade brought Gretzky to St. Louis, where the Blues took a run at the Stanley Cup by trading some prospects and draft picks to the Kings for a chance to have the Great One lead them higher. A free agent contract with the New York Rangers gave him a chance to be reunited with his longtime friend and Edmonton teammate, Mark Messier; a chance to pursue the Cup one more time on the biggest stage; and another chance to bring hockey to a larger and larger audience. No matter where he has been or will be, Gretzky's career accomplishments are unrivaled and perhaps unapproachable. 🏒 Gretzky's career now spans 17 NHL seasons. He has won 10 Art Ross Trophies as scoring champion. His playmaking magic has 14 times seen him lead the league in assists. He has six times led all scorers in Stanley Cup play, twice earning the Conn Smythe Trophy as playoff MVP. He has been named to the NHL's First or Second All-Star Team 13 times. And over the course of that amazing career, he has rewritten the NHL record book as an autobiography, having set 61 NHL single-game, one-season, and career scoring records. 🏒 Gretzky's astonishing feats of goal-scoring and playmaking are merely the most obvious evidence of his supremacy. He did not simply break records, he flew past them and out of sight, and he did it not only once but again and again and again, scaling heights undreamt of. It was as if, confronting a mountain that had daunted all but the strongest, he had strolled effortlessly to its summit and, without pausing, just kept walking into the sky, where none could follow.

*SMILE PRETTY FOR THE CAMERA-A Gretzky smile usually means trouble for the opposition.*

If any came close, it was usually because Gretzky himself had lifted them higher. Winger after winger had by far the best season of his career while serving as Gretzky's linemate; he made the mediocre good, and the good, great. "If you're going to get a guy who can make a difference, it's certainly Wayne Gretzky," said St. Louis all-star defenseman Al MacInnis, after Gretzky's February 1996 trade to the Blues. "He makes everybody around him that much better, and he has done it through his whole career."

But the Great One's contributions to hockey never stopped with his brilliance on the ice. Never the biggest, fastest, strongest, or hardest-shooting, the whippet-lean Gretzky is the epitome of the thinking man's player. He is hockey's version of a chess grandmaster, always four or five moves ahead of his opponents, seeing possibilities that no one else can see until it's too late. The very embodiment of clean, graceful play, four times awarded the Lady Byng Trophy as the game's most gentlemanly player, his strong comments against fighting and violence in hockey were diplomatic but persuasive.

Beyond that, his good looks, boyish charm, and articulate, even-tempered presence in the heat of playoff competition, in his unofficial position as spokesman for the state of hockey, in labor-management relations, or in the spotlight that has followed him throughout his personal life, have made him hockey's ambassador. This is the man who had the perfect sense of occasion, when Edmonton won the Stanley Cup the year after defenseman Steve Smith's own-goal error had eliminated the Oilers, to make sure Smith was the first teammate he passed the Cup to. And in the tumult of the Canada dressing room after the team's dramatic last-minute victory in the '86 Canada Cup, his first words before a celebrating nation were devoted to quietly wishing his grandmother a happy birthday.

His arrival in L.A., and the success to which he carried the Kings, gave hockey eminence and credibility in regions of the United States far beyond its traditionally established northern strongholds, making possible expansion to big Sun Belt cities in the 1990s. "He changed the face of hockey," said Bruce McNall, former owner of the Kings, "not only by bringing in expansion but by bringing in TV contracts with ESPN and Fox. He was instrumental in making this a major sport." It is amazing to think that at this late stage in Gretzky's career of overarching class, he had to endure criticism that he had quit on the Kings in '95-96, after it became clear that the club would be in no financial position to challenge for the Cup for some time. "I want to win," said Gretzky. "To criticize me for stepping forward to complain about mediocrity, well, for people to accept losing in life, that's not right." It was a reminder of one more thing that has made Gretzky great: his fierce devotion to competitive excellence.

Gretzky has now spent half his life as the NHL's

Gretzky's astonishing feats of goal-scoring and playmaking are obvious evidence of his supremacy in the history of hockey.

premier player, broken every noteworthy record, and long since taken his place as the all-time leader in every major statistical category. He has become like Voyager, having passed every recognizable landmark, every last milestone, now cruising onward beyond the solar system and into the uncharted reaches of deep space. His destiny is a place in the heavens among the hockey gods, the greatest of all the great players who came before him, who lived its legends and wrote its history.

Out of the mists of the game's very origin in the 19th century, some anonymous master of the game passes the puck to Russell Bowie, whose extraordinary career ended in the ECAHA of 1908, where Cyclone Taylor's began; Bowie passes to Taylor, whose phenomenal career crossed paths with Joe Malone's; Taylor dishes to Malone, the greatest goal-scorer in the dawn of the NHL, a grizzled veteran by the time King Clancy entered the league; Malone passes to Clancy, the beloved little scoring defenseman, who battled Dit Clapper for 10 years; Clancy gives it to Clapper, the big scoring winger of the Dynamite Line, who inspired Gordie Howe and whose long career was winding down as Howe's was beginning; Clapper headmans to Howe, "Mr. Hockey," the greatest scorer in NHL history until Gretzky, Gretzky's own inspiration and personal friend, still rock solid at the astounding age of 52 in his last NHL season, the teenaged Gretzky's first; Howe sends it to Gretzky, a puck passed from hockey's ancient wellspring, sent from the stick of one great to another across generations, and he is in, free and clear, carrying it to the goal, and skating on to join the immortals.

# Paul Kariya

PITY THE PLAYER BURDENED WITH THE LABEL "THE NEXT WAYNE GRETZKY." IT'S HARD ENOUGH TO COME into the NHL and do well in your first couple of years, but to have to lug around that deadweight of impossible expectations on your back?...  Well, one player has been burdened with that label, and he has borne up under it with enviable poise—Gretzkylike poise, you might say. That player is Paul Kariya of the Mighty Ducks of Anaheim, a team not merely headquartered just down the freeway from Gretzky's longtime *locus vivendi*, but one that owes its very existence to the Sun Belt hockey boom Gretzky wrought. From the moment Kariya first pulled on a Mighty Ducks' sweater and skated out before his team's enthusiastic fans—9,000 of whom showed up to watch his debut at an open practice—he has had to contend with the notion that he is the Next Gretzky.  "Everybody has their little game making comparisons," he says. "I know who I am. I'm Paul Kariya." And Kariya is very much his own man—a darting, dancing left winger whose bouts of improbably creative playmaking seem like flights of fancy, yet are actually the result of rigorous planning and practice, practice, practice.  In his first NHL season, the abbreviated 1995 campaign, he led all rookies in goal-scoring. In his second year, he tied for seventh in scoring among all league players, spearheaded the Ducks' late-season surge, and even did some key scouting that, in essence, put Anaheim on the hockey map. Not a bad two years for a quiet 21-year-old.  Not that Kariya is a stranger to momentous events on the hockey rink. After two years of racking up high scoring and low penalty-minute totals in the British Columbia Tier II junior league, the North Vancouver native traveled east to matriculate at the University of Maine. There, his 93 points in 36 regular-season games, good for a 2.6 per-game average, set an NCAA record as he led the Black Bears to the NCAA final. Kariya's assists on all three of Maine's unanswered third-period goals in the championship game gave the school a 5-4 victory and its first-ever national title. He crowned his season by becoming the first freshman ever to win the Hobey Baker Award as U.S. college hockey's player of the year.  But that's not all the 5-10, 165-pound whippet did in 1992-93. He also played for Canada in the World Junior Championships, helping his country win gold and being chosen as a tournament all-star. He then played for Canada at the World Championships, finishing fourth on the team in scoring despite being the first nondrafted teenager ever to play in that tourney.  He didn't remain undrafted after that caliber of season. Anaheim took him with the fourth pick overall. But he elected not to sign so he could play for his country

*HELP-All Anaheim's Paul Kariya needs now is a team-mate to put the puck in the open net.*

once more, at the '94 Olympics. Kariya's experience at Lillehammer was bittersweet. He led Canada in scoring with seven points in eight Olympic games, including an overtime marker against the Czech Republic that lifted the Canadians to the semifinals. But when the final against Sweden ended with the score 2-2, Olympic rules dictated that the game be decided through the contrived melodrama of a penalty-shot contest. After Peter Forsberg beat Corey Hirsch to put Sweden ahead in the shootout, it all came down to Kariya. He went high on Sweden goalie Tommy Salo, but Salo stopped it. Thus Sweden took the gold, Canada the silver.

"As time goes on, the more grateful and thankful I will be for what we accomplished," said Kariya long afterward. "But I still think of what

could have been. I've gone over that penalty shot 200 times in my head, trying to change it."

Kariya couldn't change it, so he did the next best thing. Two months later he propelled Canada to the gold at the World Championships by notching a team-high 12 points in eight games, even though he was the youngest player on the roster. He was named the tournament's top forward.

Now he was ready to sign with the Ducks, sparking the Kariyamania that manifested itself at that first open practice. He immediately impressed teammates with his maturity and humility. "The way I am right now is due to the way my parents raised me," said Kariya, who has an interesting background. Both his parents are schoolteachers. His mother, Sharon, is Scottish; his father, Tetsuhiko, was born of Japanese parents in a World War II internment camp in Canada and went on to play for the Canadian national rugby team. They imbued in their son the values of deference, responsibility, and intellectual curiosity. "That's what makes Paul so different," said Anaheim coach Ron Wilson. "He's normal."

Normal—but intense. In an effort to sharpen his powers of concentration, Kariya read self-improvement books and repeatedly visualized moves he would make on the ice. Ex-Maine teammate Jim Montgomery reported that when Kariya made some heretofore unprecedented feint, "I think it's something he's already seen, already done many times in his mind, maybe 10, maybe 50 times. When he does it, it looks new, but to him, it isn't." Seeking that extra edge in hand-eye coordination, Kariya even taught himself how to juggle.

In the 47 games of his first NHL season, he logged 18 goals, tops among all rookies, and 39 points, good for No. 2 behind his old tormentor, Forsberg. Kariya probably would've beaten out Forsberg for the Calder Trophy had it not been for his team-worst minus-17 rating, an aberration for Kariya, whose junior, college, and international ratings were all well into plus.

Having bulked up for his sophomore season to a somewhat more muscular 5-11 and 175 pounds, Kariya also tried to lighten up mentally. He no longer obsessed over his sticks—in his rookie year he'd spend hours with a blowtorch, trying to fashion the perfect curve for each stick blade—and started to engage in his first tentative banter with teammates. "Last year we used to rib him and he used to smile like he was almost biting his

®& © Mighty Ducks

T hat's what makes Paul so different. He's normal.

lip," said defenseman Bobby Dollas.

Chosen to play in the midseason All-Star Game, Kariya responded with a goal and an assist, despite his awe at playing on a line with Gretzky—whom he calls "untouchable, incomparable"—and Brett Hull. "I was sitting next to Gretzky and Hull," said Kariya. "I pinched myself. Those are the guys I idolized growing up." (Indeed, Kariya's mother revealed that when Paul was a boy, he so idolized Gretzky that when Gretzky was traded from Edmonton to Los Angeles in 1988, "he absolutely refused to believe it. To this day, when he comes home from school or wherever he's been, he puts on tapes of Wayne Gretzky.")

But Kariya was not too awed to note the abundant skills of a Western Conference teammate, Winnipeg's Teemu Selanne. Kariya returned to Anaheim and convinced general manager Jack Ferreira to acquire the talented Finnish Flash.

The Kariya-Selanne combination instantly became one of hockey's most electrifying partnerships, and the Ducks went on a 17-9-3 tear that left them a single point shy of the final playoff berth. Nevertheless, notice had been served. Anaheim was a force to be reckoned with—and so was Kariya, who in only his second NHL season had scored an emphatic 50 goals and 58 assists, improved his rating to plus-9, and won the Lady Byng Trophy.

"The next Wayne Gretzky?" Perhaps. But if this keeps up, pretty soon those comparisons will be passé. Instead, some young player somewhere is going to have to deal with his own burden—that of being labeled "the next Paul Kariya."

# Mario Lemieux

MARIO LEMIEUX HAS PROVIDED US WITH SO MANY INDELIBLE MEMORIES: THE HUNDREDS OF BEAUTIFUL GOALS and gorgeous assists, the countless breathtaking plays that left us doubting the possibility of what we just saw, the image of the big, unstoppable center gliding down the ice, opposing defensemen strewn behind him like children fallen off an accelerating toboggan, deftly sweeping the puck from side to side at the end of his weaving stick, slipping the disk past a beached and flailing goalie, flashing a bright smile at his teammates as he arcs past the boards, hands held skyward. Over and over he's given us these scenes of power and grace and glory, and that would've been more than enough for any fan. ⬤ But Lemieux, improbably, has provided us still more. He has been stricken with cancer and a debilitating series of spinal injuries, dealt with both with exemplary courage and poise, and somehow emerged as inconceivably great as ever. Among the all-time greats, only Bobby Orr, playing on crippled knees, and Gordie Howe, surviving a life-threatening skull fracture, had to endure something approaching the extreme physical adversity that Lemieux has had to go through while maintaining an Olympian level of play. ⬤ Flash back to March 2, 1993. Lemieux undergoes the last of four weeks worth of daily radiation treatments to battle the Hodgkin's disease diagnosed in his lymph nodes. The Pittsburgh superstar lies in a high-energy linear accelerator, beneath a face mask and lead shield designed to protect his vital organs from massive radiation doses 50 times stronger than a normal X-ray, and receives his final blast—one so strong it actually burns a spot on his neck. That night, Lemieux is given a 90-second standing ovation as he strides onto the ice at the Spectrum in Philadelphia for his first game since January. Incredibly, he scores a goal and an assist. Even more incredibly, he will go on to notch back-to-back four-goal games, a five-goal game, run Buffalo's Pat LaFontaine down from behind to win his fourth scoring title with 160 points in only 60 games, record a league-leading plus-55 rating, and, not incidentally, lead the Penguins to their first-ever regular-season championship. It is believed by many to be the most amazing single-season performance of all time. ⬤ Lemieux's Hodgkin's went into remission, where it remains to this day. But his '93-94 season was cut short due to recurring back problems and an anemic condition that is a frequent consequence of radiation therapy. Finally, after sitting out the '94-95 campaign to recover his strength and decide whether he was willing and physically able to return to the demanding world of professional hockey, he came back—again. ⬤ Flash back once more, to the Pittsburgh Civic Arena, October 7, 1995.

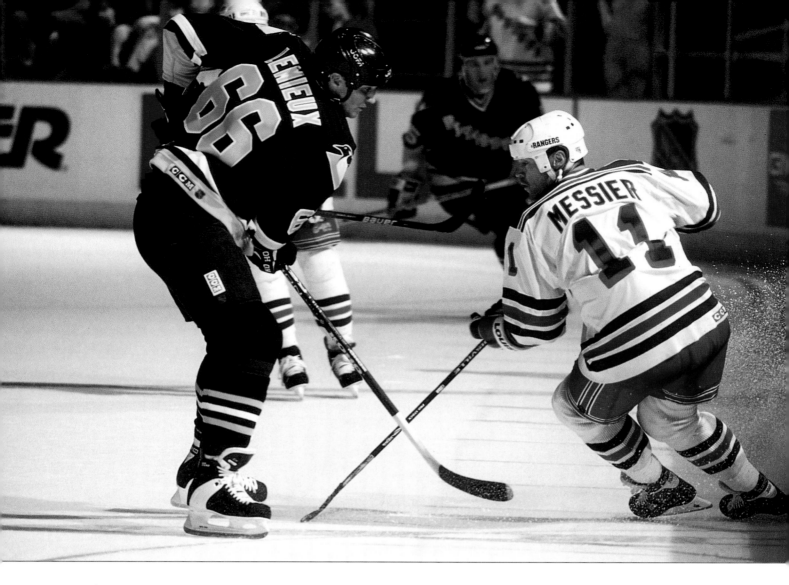

*TOUCHÉ-Penguins captain Mario Lemieux and Rangers captain Mark Messier duel for position.*

Lemieux steps onto the ice to exploding indoor fireworks and another huge ovation, then records four assists to lead the Pens to a one-sided win over Toronto. In November he pots four goals in Boston—and the Bruins' fans give him a standing ovation. "They don't do that," says Pittsburgh coach Eddie Johnston, who spent most of his playing career as a Bruins' goalie, of the Boston fans. "That just tells you they acknowledged the best player in the game today." By midseason, Lemieux feels fatigued. "I'm tired all the time, and it shows in my performance on the ice," he says following a three-game stretch in which he tallies nine points and

leads the NHL in scoring by a dozen. We should all be so tired.

And so there promises to be more thrills from the player who has supplied them to fans since he was a four-year-old growing up in the Ville Emard section of Montreal. Lemieux got his start playing in midwinter with his parents and two brothers in the family living room, where all doors and windows were occasionally left open and snow packed down on the old carpet to supply an intimate, if unusual, indoor minirink. From this odd beginning, Lemieux's skills quickly took root. By the time he was six, his youth league games drew as many as 5,000 fans. At age

12, then-Canadiens coach Scotty Bowman called him the greatest prospect he had ever seen.

Lemieux would go on to shatter all Canadian junior scoring records and, after being drafted by the Penguins for the '84–85 campaign, save that flagging franchise and help turn it into one of the league's most successful. But his long, loping strides and phlegmatic style—in which he punished foes who slashed and hacked at him not by hitting back with fists or bodychecks, but by scoring goal after goal after goal—led many to believe he wasn't trying all that hard. Even after piling up 145 goals and 203 assists in his first three years and winning the Hart and Ross trophies in his fourth, some hockey commentators called Lemieux a floater. True, Lemieux smoked cigarettes as a teenager and never worked out with weights till he reached age 30, his only off-ice exercise consisting of honing his prodigious golf skills. Asked once if he worked out during the summer, Lemieux replied, "Yeah. Starting August 1, I don't order french fries with my sandwich."

However unconventional his training regimen, Lemieux's competitive fire has always burned fierce and hot. Playing alongside Wayne Gretzky in a dream combination, he single-handedly won the 1987 Canada Cup for his nation by scoring the last three goals, including the overtime winner, against the USSR in one game, then captured the final with a masterful last-minute wrist shot. He strung together a near-record 46-game point-scoring streak in '89–90 while in agony from a herniated disk, then developed an even more painful post-operation spinal infection that kept him out till January 1991—and promptly

I'm tired all the time," he says, following a three-game stretch in which he tallies nine points. We should all be so tired.

scored three assists in his first game back. He led the Pens to the Cup that year with an astounding 44 points in 23 playoff games, despite back woes so severe a trainer had to tie Lemieux's skates each night to spare him the agony of bending over. Lemieux did it again in '92, as the Pens won a second straight Cup while he won a second straight Conn Smythe Trophy, despite missing five games with a broken hand after being slashed by a Ranger. In light of all that, it seems absurd that anyone ever questioned his commitment to the game.

A quiet man, Lemieux closely guards his privacy. Not many knew that a point-a-game "slump" late in the '95–96 season was caused by his concern over his wife's difficult pregnancy with their third child. But two nights after the baby was successfully delivered, Lemieux celebrated by scoring five goals and two assists against St. Louis. He is now recognized by many as hockey's premier player of the '90s—and, if he keeps it up for another four or five more years, perhaps of all time. Yet it beggars the imagination to think of how much more Lemieux could have done had illness and injury not intervened. "I'm not coming back to be an average player," he said when he returned, at age 30, for the third comeback of his career. "I want to come back and be one of the top players in the world."

Super Mario. Mario le Magnifique. These are some of the nicknames by which he is known. But if you want to find the best description for this incomparable player, all you need do is translate his last name from the French. Lemieux: it means the best.

# Eric Lindros

THEY USED TO SAY THAT IF WAYNE GRETZKY IS THE GREAT ONE AND MARIO LEMIEUX THE MAGNIFICENT ONE, then surely Eric Lindros is the Next One. Well, they can't say that anymore, because Big No. 88's time is now here. 🏒 You might say it arrived on February 9, 1995, the day left wing John LeClair was acquired from Montreal, forging the last link in the gigantic Legion of Doom line—6-4 Canadian Lindros at center; 6-2 American LeClair on the left side; 6-2 Swede Mikael Renberg on the right—that has terrorized NHL opponents since the day it was formed. At the time of that trade the Flyers were 3-7-1 and threatening to miss the playoffs a sixth straight year. Lindros, despite his own superlative record in his first two-plus NHL seasons, was depressed ("I was afraid of being a bust," he remembers. "I was getting hurt all the time—knees, shoulder—and I wasn't on a strong team. I had trouble dealing with it."). But after the trade the Flyers went 25-9-3, roared through two playoff rounds before finally falling in the semifinals, and rumbled into a future so bright they had to wear shades. The punishing 230-pounder with the soft scoring touch wound up the year accepting the MVP trophy at the NHL's postseason awards show, breaking down in tears as he expressed his gratitude to his family. 🏒 But with the status and respect the imposing Lindros now enjoys as hockey's signature superstar, there comes a terrible burden of expectation as well. After his Flyers were bounced from the playoffs two years running by workmanlike, superstarless teams—the New Jersey Devils in '95, the Florida Panthers in '96—his leadership skills were questioned by some. Never mind that Lindros was one of the youngest captains in NHL history (he was given his first "C" at age 21), or that it took Gretzky five years and Lemieux seven to win their first Cups (the '96-97 season will only be his fifth). Lindros's successes as a teen phenom were so frequent and dominant that anything less today seems like a disappointment. 🏒 And what successes they were: At age 16 he led his team to the Ontario Junior B championship, then scored at a monstrous four-points-a-game clip in Tier II play—then collected a gold medal as the youngest player at the 1990 World Junior Championships. 🏒 At age 17 he amassed 18 goals and 18 assists in 17 playoff games to lead the Oshawa Generals to the Memorial Cup, Canada's major junior title. 🏒 At age 18 he piled up 71 goals and 78 assists in just 57 games for Oshawa, then notched 17 points in seven games to lead Canada to an unprecedented second straight World Junior crown—then, made the Canada Cup squad, knocked Sweden's hulking Ulf Samuelsson out of the tournament with a titanic body check, and, despite being the only amateur on the team,

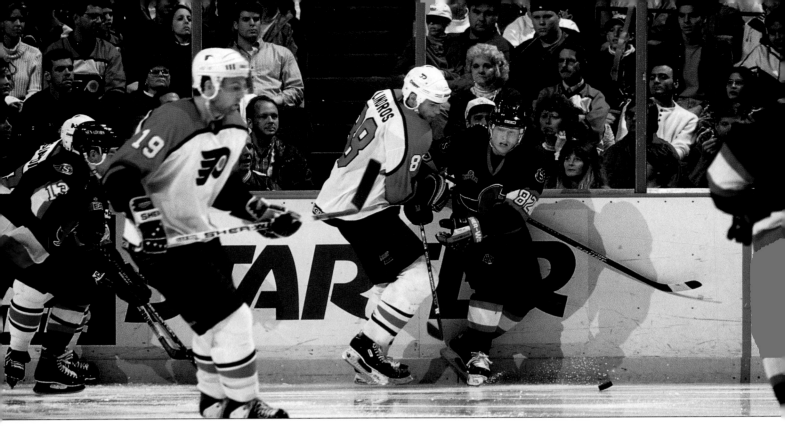

*BROTHERLY LOVE-
Playing with Eric Lindros
has been a* boon *for teammate Mikael Renberg's
career. And playing
against Eric has been
a* boom *for others.*

contributed six points to his country's eight-game triumph.

Still 18, his 11 points in eight games led Canada to a silver medal at the 1992 Olympics—the country's best hockey performance at the winter games in 32 years.

That completed perhaps the most incredible run of honors ever put together by one player in a concentrated period of time, as Lindros crashed opponents into the boards, steamrolled them in open ice, smeared them into oily smudges in horribly one-sided collisions. He intimidated with his fists and his glowering stare, and even when he was the deferential young cub among Team Canada's seasoned pros, he had no trouble keeping up with Gretzky, Lemieux, and Mark Messier, the hard-hitting leader he took as a role model.

"Eric could turn around the entire tempo of a game without even touching the puck," remembers Team Canada forward Brendan Shanahan.

"It's like, 'Here I am. I'm coming. My elbows are down and I'm going to run you over.' It was a head-on challenge—and Eric won them all."

But if such spectacular achievements enthralled a continent, there was another, highly controversial side to the young giant's saga. The Nordiques made Lindros the No. 1 pick overall in 1991, even though he had already insisted he did not want to play in Quebec. When Lindros refused to sign, many observers branded him a selfish whiner—and in French Canada, he was labeled a bigot. *L'affaire Lindros* soon became a bitter national debate, a tableau in miniature of Canada's age-old clash between anglophone and francophone.

Lindros maintained that his refusal was merely about not wanting to play in a small, isolated market with what was then a chronically losing team. Any "talk about me being anti-French," he said, was "bull. I think it's great that the people of

Quebec have a different heritage. Diversity is great." Still, he and his tight-knit family stood firm against the Nordiques, with the strongest public statements coming from Lindros's mother (who, in Eric's junior days, had nixed her son's move to faraway Sault Sainte Marie, Ontario, when that team acquired his rights). Anti-Lindros sentiment in Quebec escalated. When he appeared in the province with the national team, fans scorned him as a mama's boy and bombarded him with pacifiers.

Lindros endured the abuse manfully and maintained his amateur status for one year, forcing the Nords to trade him or lose his rights altogether. On June 20, 1992, the last possible day for Quebec to act, an agitated Nordiques president Marcel Aubut traded Lindros—twice. It later took an arbitrator's ruling to confirm that the youthful behemoth had been dealt to Philadelphia—not New York—in exchange for forwards Mike Ricci, Peter Forsberg, and Chris Simon, goaler Ron Hextall, defensemen Steve Duchesne and Kerry Huffman, two first-round draft choices, and $15 million.

The deal redeemed Lindros—"the guy who behaved all along like the responsible adult," wrote a Toronto columnist, "was the teenager"—and made the Flyers instant Stanley Cup contenders. Despite a spate of injuries that his ultraphysical style leaves him prone to, Lindros racked up 75 points in 61 games his rookie year, 97 points in 65 games his sophomore year, and big plus marks to go along with them. The Spectrum, quiet for so many years while the Flyers struggled, was once again the seething cauldron it had been during its Broad Street

Eric could turn around the entire tempo of a game without even touching the puck.

Bullies heyday. Everywhere you looked on the streets of Philadelphia, someone was wearing a No. 88 sweater in orange and black.

In the shortened '95 season, the man teammate Craig MacTavish called "an absolute hockey *machine*" was headed to his first-ever NHL scoring crown when he was hit in the eye by a rebounding puck. Lindros missed the last two games of the season, and Pittsburgh's Jaromir Jagr passed him for the Art Ross Trophy on the final day.

In '95-96 Lindros's 115 points in 73 games propelled the Flyers to first place in the East. But after Philly fell to Florida in six second-round games, people started asking questions. Why, when the going got rough against the Devils and Panthers, did Lindros seem to grow sullen rather than fiery? Would he ever outgrow his penchant for taking needless, chippy penalties at key moments? Is the big, nasty, steamroller type of player that Lindros epitomizes really the wave of the future, or is the NHL's prototype for the 21st century to be found in shifty speed demons like Joe Sakic, Sergei Federov, and Teemu Selanne?

Such questions must remain unanswered for now. But in the meantime, Lindros and his Legionnaires of Doom continue to gather experience, absorbing the setbacks every great must suffer before ascending the plinth of glory, where at last they can drink from the Stanley Cup. He has already taken the Flyers a long way in a short time, and he is still young, his potential limitless. In many ways he is still a young boy skating on his backyard rink.

"We are supposed to be grown men, mature guys," says Lindros, "but in our hearts, we are kids, having fun, playing a game that we love."

# Mark Messier

WHEN MARK MESSIER WALKS INTO THE DRESSING ROOM AFTER A GAME—A GAME IN WHICH HE HAS usually scored or set up at least one vital goal, or jarred at least one opponent with a clattering bodycheck—everything stops. TV cameras, microphones, and cassette recorders sprout in a kind of penumbra around his bullet-taut head, and Messier, the greatest team leader in sports today, speaks. He praises underrated teammates or deflects blame from those who happened to falter, always choosing the right words to keep the club running smoothly. His legendary piercing gaze is tempered for the setting, but still his eyes laser in on each reporter as he answers. Finally, after thanking everyone, the Ranger captain turns his chiseled body back to the training room to rejoin his mates. It is a masterful performance, repeated night after night, and it reinforces the tales of Messier's indomitable behind-the-scenes leadership that have filtered out over the years: how he cornered an underperforming player on a team flight and threatened to toss him out the door if he didn't start giving 100 percent; how he took a talented but raw young defenseman by the name of Brian Leetch under his wing and nurtured him into a star; how he constructively challenged Rangers coach Mike Keenan when the team faltered in the '94 playoffs, and fell weeping in Keenan's arms from the emotional strain; how he has organized impromptu team dinners, parties, and vacations that relieved tension, built morale, and earned him the respect and love of his fellow players. And that's off the ice. What Messier has done on the ice over the nearly two decades of his incredible career is known to all: Two Hart Trophy seasons, a Conn Smythe Trophy, two First Team All-Star selections at center and two more at left wing; 1,468 regular-season points through the '95-96 season, placing him fifth on the all-time NHL list; 106 career playoff goals, 177 assists, and 283 points, second behind his close friend Wayne Gretzky in each category on the all-time postseason list; and, most important of all, his name on the Stanley Cup six times—five times as an Edmonton Oiler, once as a New York Ranger. In the '96-97 season, these two superstar friends will be reunited, as Rangers, to skate for the Cup again. And yet, despite his massive exploits on the rink, Messier's reputation as a leader of men is so great it threatens to overshadow all the goals scored, all the faceoffs won, all the opponents leveled. Take his most famous feat, in the 1994 semifinals against New Jersey, three years after the Rangers acquired him to end their long Stanley Cup drought. With New York headed to the Meadowlands facing elimination and his teammates needing an emotional lift, Messier guaranteed victory before a gaggle of reporters:

"We know we are going to go in there and win Game 6 and bring it back to the Garden."

But after two periods the Rangers trailed, 2-1. So Messier took matters into his own hands, scoring three unanswered third-period goals to win the game—a performance that ranks in New York sports legend alongside Babe Ruth's called shot and Joe Namath's Super Bowl guarantee. "He leads," noted the Devils' Bernie Nicholls, "and they follow." Two weeks later, after he scored what turned out to be the Cup-winning goal in Game 7 of the Final, Messier flashed a thousand-watt smile as he hoisted Lord Stanley's coveted goblet—the first time any Ranger had done it in 54 years. "All the ghosts," said the Rangers' messiah. "All the bad luck for this organization. Nineteen-forty, rest in peace."

It was not the first time the Edmonton native had accomplished the impossible. He broke into the pros at seventeen with Indianapolis and Cincinnati of the old World Hockey Association, then joined Gretzky and the rest of the cocky young Edmonton Oilers in 1979-80. Those swashbucklers scored and partied like madmen for four years, then, as experienced veterans in their mid-twenties, won Stanley Cups in 1984, '85, '87, and '88. The debate raged: Was the Oilers' success due to Gretzky, their captain and the most awesome scorer the game had ever seen, or was Messier, who consistently registered 100-point seasons despite playing on another line entirely, just as responsible?

The question was answered in 1990, two years after Gretzky had been dealt to Los Angeles. Messier, the Oilers his team now, crafted his finest season ever—45 goals and 129 points—then

Fearless doesn't begin to describe Messier. He's not only fearless, he's downright scary.

added 31 points in 22 playoff games. When the Oilers clinched the Final at Northlands Coliseum, he grabbed the Cup, skated over to the glass at the corner of the rink, and held it aloft so the hometown fans, all his friends and neighbors, could exult with him. The *Hockey News* published a photo of that indelible moment on its cover with the entirely appropriate single-word headline: "REDEMPTION."

Messier was indeed redeemed, although no one would dare tell him to his face that he needed redeeming. Mean (he has been suspended four times for injuring opponents with stick fouls), still capable of getting into the occasional fight, and more than willing to throw an elbow at any opponent in his way, number 11 is the consummate physical player, the natural successor to Gordie Howe and precursor to Eric Lindros.

There are many hockey people who would rate him with Gretzky and Lemieux. Messier, after all, has won as many Stanley Cups as those two combined, and was every bit as instrumental in leading the Canadian national team to victory in the '84, '87, and '91 Canada Cups. When Messier arrived at Team Canada's '91 training camp, starting goalie and ex-Oilers teammate Bill Ranford simply said, "Well, there he is. There's our fearless leader." Adds Lindros, who as a teen kept a hockey card of his idol in his wallet, "Fearless doesn't begin to describe Messier. He's not only fearless, he's downright scary."

But not entirely scary. *Sports Illustrated* once aptly described him as "half-man, half-Easter Island statue" with eyes that "can smelt iron ore," yet Messier, who lives in a Manhattan townhouse, is also cerebral and reflective. "There is

nothing more beautiful," he says, "than twenty, twenty-five guys thinking the same way and going out and winning. I've won six times, and the Cup becomes part of your soul. It's not on a conscious level—know what I mean?—but it becomes who you are. Not your philosophy but part of your everyday being."

In the end, Messier leads by imparting a code of compassion, obligation, and dignity. He is a key figure in the Players Association (his father, Doug, co-founded the first-ever hockey players union back in the mid-'60s). After the Rangers won the Cup, he brought it to the hospital bed of a thirteen-year-old boy awaiting a heart transplant; seven months later, that boy sat on the bench when Messier and the Rangers raised their championship banner.

It is through these truly remarkable qualities that Mark Messier has earned the respect and admiration of most everyone he has come into contact with. "You think of Patton," says Rangers goalie Glenn Healy, "you think of MacArthur . . . that's how we feel about Mark."

And, indeed, it is how everyone in hockey thinks of Mark Messier, the greatest team leader in sports today.

*AND THEY'RE OFF-Mark Messier is in the lead as the chase for the puck begins.*

# Patrick Roy

ANYONE WHO'S WORKED FOR YEARS ACHIEVING EXCELLENCE AT HIS JOB, EARNING ACCLAIM AND RESPECT AND the perks that go with it, only to get a new boss who tries to take it all away and looks for an opportunity to embarrass him, had to identify just a little with Patrick Roy last season. And no matter who the fans were pulling for in the Stanley Cup playoffs, they had to take some satisfaction in Roy's performance, as he led the Colorado Avalanche to the Cup, and to whatever personal vindication he needed.  Roy has been one of the NHL's premier goaltenders ever since coming out of Granby in the Quebec Junior League. The Montreal Canadiens' fourth-round pick in the 1984 Entry Draft, Roy became the Habs' number one netminder during the 1985-1986 NHL campaign. A natural butterfly-style goalie who adopted a stand-up style, the Ste. Foy, Quebec, native was named to the league's all-rookie team despite an unimpressive freshman year. It was in that season's playoffs, though, that Roy made his mark. Just twenty years old and coming off his first full NHL season, the unheralded Roy sparkled in the nets, posting a stupendous .923 save percentage, leading an unprepossessing Canadiens team to the Stanley Cup and earning the Conn Smythe Trophy as playoff MVP. "I haven't seen goaltending like that in fourteen years," said Larry Robinson, Montreal's great veteran defenseman. Roy was adamant about spreading the credit around to his teammates. As to the poise and brilliance of his own performance, "The key," said Roy, was that "my coach had confidence in me that I could do the job." Roy's success only continued. While his eccentricities were frequently noted—the wiry six-footer often looked nervous and uncomfortable in the crease, talked to the goalposts during stoppages to keep himself focused, and made such a habit of flexing his neck to stay loose that he was nicknamed "The Goose"—they never overshadowed the praise for his outstanding play. Playing behind a defense-minded team, Roy annually has been among the NHL's leaders in goals-against average; he shared the Jennings Trophy, awarded to the team allowing the fewest goals, three straight years from 1987 to '89, and won it outright in '92. More important, he has usually been among the NHL's leaders in save percentage, earning awards and honors that piled up: three times named to the NHL's First All-Star Team, twice chosen for the Second Team, selected six times to appear in the All-Star Game, and three times voted the Vezina Trophy as the best netminder in the National Hockey League. His style has evolved, too, reverting more to a flopping, butterfly method, but also playing the angles better; one of Roy's most important skills is the ability to absorb the hardest shots, rarely giving up a big rebound.

In 1989 Roy again carried Montreal to the Stanley Cup Final; in spite of his superb .920 save percentage and playoff-leading 2.09 goals-against mark, Les Habs fell in six games to powerhouse Calgary. Four years later, Roy led the Canadiens back, and he was even better, smothering playoff opponents with a stunning .929 efficiency and 2.13 goals-against figure. In one of those subtle moments that become the stuff of Stanley Cup legend, Roy stopped a dangerous Los Angeles flurry around the net in Game 4 of the Final, pinned the puck in the crease, looked up at Kings' chippy winger Tomas Sandstrom—and winked. "I just wanted to show him that I was tough," chuckled Roy. Ten times taken into sudden-death overtime, Montreal, with Roy between the pipes, won every one of those games; the bleu, blanc, et rouge lost only four games in four post-season rounds, and the Cup was again at home in the Montreal Forum. "Patrick Roy was simply outstanding," said Jacques Demers, the coach who masterminded a hundred-point season and a Cup triumph with a star goalie and a collection of unheralded players. "He was dominating." Roy won the Smythe Trophy for the second time.

You'd think that, like Demers, most coaches would thank their lucky stars to have a goaltender with a resume as long and impressive as Roy's, and would do what they could to keep him happy. But even after a century of hockey, the art of goaltending—its value, its measurement, its mental dimension—is still poorly understood and rarely appreciated by many

> Patrick is the first real bona fide superstar with a presence that we've had in our organization.

coaches and managers. That misunderstanding and a clash of egos led to the biggest flap of the 1995-96 NHL season.

The Canadiens, Roy included, were awful as the season began, resulting in impatient front-office firings and the installation of former Canadiens winger Mario Tremblay as Montreal's new coach. Although he and Tremblay did not belong to a mutual fan club, Roy lifted his statistics back into the NHL's upper echelons and was the cardinal reason for Montreal's surge back to the .500 level. But on December 2, they hosted a juggernaut Detroit side that was on the road to the league record for victories in a season, and the Red Wings showed no mercy. Neither did Tremblay, nor the Montreal fans. As the score mounted, Forum faithful razzed Roy with a Bronx cheer after an easy save; he challenged them with a conquering upward thrust of his arms. The onslaught continued, and Tremblay would not rescue Roy from what had become a stint in a carnival dunk-tank, until Detroit made it 9-1 halfway through the game. Humiliated, Roy paced back and forth on the Montreal bench, vowing it would be his last game for the Canadiens. It was. Rather than smoothing things over, the Canadiens traded Roy to their former Quebec rivals, the Colorado Avalanche.

"He has come in and given us a presence," said Avs' coach Marc Crawford. "You hear about what superstars like Mark Messier and Mario Lemieux do for teams, and Patrick is the first real bona fide superstar with a presence that we've had in our organization. Peter [Forsberg] and Joe [Sakic] are superstars, but

they don't have that same presence that really has an effect on the whole team."

Roy stopped 37 of 39 Canadiens' shots in a 5-2 win when he faced his old team a few weeks later. "I think every athlete has pride," said Roy, "and when you face your ex-team, you always want to do well—you want to show that your new team made a good deal with you."

That was an understatement. The Canadiens' season ended in April, knocked out in the first round of the playoffs. With Roy playing every game in net, compiling a .921 save percentage and 2.10 goals-against average, Colorado won the Stanley Cup.

"Even though I'm not in Montreal, the objective is still the same," says Roy. "It's winning at the end."

*A MODEL OF EXCELLENCE-Colorado's Patrick Roy displays the form that has made him one of the most successful goaltenders in League history.*

# Joe Sakic

OF ALL THE STRANGE TURNS OF FATE SPORT HAS TAKEN OVER THE DECADES, NONE CAN HAVE BEEN MORE strangely bittersweet than the one that befell Quebec fans in 1995-96—the year their beloved Nordiques pulled up stakes after 23 years in the capital city and, as the Colorado Avalanche, won the Stanley Cup. Outside Quebec, in anglophone Canada and in the United States, this progression of events was seen as little more than a mildly cruel irony—another example of Yankee hijacking of the True North's native sport, perhaps, or of hockey's healthy spread to new locales. Quebec was the ultimate "small market," incapable of supporting an NHL team not only by its modest population and the relative weakness of Canadian currency, but by its language. Beyond the Ottawa River, then, Quebec's loss of the Nordiques was not generally regarded as a great loss. But the Quebeçois—and true hockey fans across Canada, the United States, and around the world—know different: the Nords' departure cost hockey one of its most emotionally resonant touchstones, a terrible cultural loss for a game whose patrimony is rooted forever in French North America. The Nordiques were not just any team. They were a founding, stable, cup-winning member of the old World Hockey Association. Both in the WHA and the NHL they consciously chose and, for a long time, maintained a strongly pro-francophone stance, preferring to hire French Canadian players and staff, even as so many other NHL teams tended to prefer hiring English Canadians. They brought the Stastnys to Quebec, spearheading the internationalist movement that revolutionized hockey on this continent, and they hosted the unforgettable Rendez-Vous '87. Within a few short years they created North America's most intense sports rivalry, with none other than the venerable Montreal Canadiens. They plummeted miserably into last place, yet still rose from those ashes to become an exciting, flashy, successful young side ready to challenge for the Stanley Cup. And at that very moment, the Nordiques left Quebec. No player more aptly embodies this strange trajectory than Joe Sakic, the quiet, hard-working, yet spectacular centerman with the deadly accurate shot; for years the superstar no one ever heard of; for four seasons the captain of French Canada's team who declined to learn the language; the winner of the 1996 Conn Smythe Trophy and sine qua non of the Colorado Avalanche's '96 Cup run. Sakic grew up in Burnaby, British Columbia, the son of Croatian immigrants, and excelled, but did not dominate, in youth hockey. Upon arriving in the Western Hockey

*SLAPSHOT-Colorado's Joe Sakic has one of the hardest and most accurate shots in the game.*

League with the Swift Current Broncos, however, he blossomed. "The first 10 minutes of the first scrimmage," remembers Graham James, his coach in juniors, "you could tell he was going to be a great player." In his two years in Swift Current, Sakic rolled up an awesome 138 goals and 155 assists in just 136 games, plus another 25 points in 14 postseason matches. His junior career was capped in 1988, when he

was named Canadian Major Junior Player of the Year.

That fall, Sakic joined the Nordiques, who had just begun a dubious streak of five consecutive seasons out of the playoffs. The 5-11, 185-pounder immediately made his presence felt, scoring nearly a point a game in his rookie year, following that with two 100-point campaigns—all while collecting just 75 penalty minutes in 230 games. Clearly, Sakic was no ordinary Joe, yet he got very little press.

"Maybe it's because he was stuck up there in Quebec," Chicago star Jeremy Roenick speculated many years later, "or his team was stuck in the doldrums, but there's not a question he's one of the most underrated players."

Sakic has no problem with his lack of fame. He attributes it to the Nords' long streak of futility. "The spotlight is on in the playoffs," he said in 1996, "and if you haven't been there, you're not going to get noticed."

Sakic toiled out of the playoff spotlight in two of the next three years. Finally, in the abbreviated 1995 campaign, the Nordiques became a competent, exciting team. After six frustrating years with the club—in which he had recorded a whopping 564 points in 461 games—Sakic was rewarded with Quebec's first-place finish in the Eastern Conference, and he himself finished fourth in the NHL scoring race. But in the playoffs it was the same old story. The inexperienced Nords fell in the first round to the defending Cup champion Rangers, and Sakic was again consigned to the anonymity of defeat.

Soon thereafter, it was announced that the Nordiques would move to Denver, and in the American West, Sakic found, things were not quite the same. "In Quebec everybody knew you," he said. "It was like we were the city's team. So we were popular and everybody knew us wherever we went. In Denver, it has been different." By the end of the season, of course, no one in Denver had any trouble recognizing Sakic. He racked up 51 goals and 69 assists—

In Quebec everybody knew you. It was like we were the city's team.

his best season ever—and finished third in the league in scoring. He and young Swedish sensation Peter Forsberg, centering different lines, gave the Avalanche a one-two punch exceeded only by Pittsburgh, whose Mario Lemieux and Jaromir Jagr were the only NHLers to score more points than the Colorado duo.

And in the playoffs, the whole hockey world finally got to see the Joe Sakic Quebec fans had watched for years: the man whose lightning acceleration instantaneously created odd-man rushes and breakaways. In the first round he turned the Vancouver series by tying Game 5 with six minutes left, then scoring the overtime winner; he won the series one game later with a 58th-minute, tie-breaking marker. In the second round he knotted the Chicago series by scoring in the third overtime period of Game 4. He broke open Game 6 of the semifinal clincher against Detroit with two goals and an assist, and in Game 3 of the Cup Final against Florida his breakaway tally gave the Avs a 3-2 victory and an unbeatable 3-0 series lead. In the end, Sakic scored 18 goals in 22 playoff games—one shy of the NHL record—and his league-leading 34 points was 12 better than the next closest Av.

Most important of all, his name was on the Stanley Cup. But for Quebec fans, fate had indeed taken a strange, bittersweet turn. Joe Sakic and the Quebec Nordiques had finally come of age—only they had done so one year, two thousand miles, and a language and culture away.

# Brendan Shanahan

"I PLAY WITH HEART," SAYS BRENDAN SHANAHAN, "AND SOMETIMES I WEAR IT ON MY SLEEVE TOO MUCH." No one would disagree, and few would want him to change. Shanahan is among the best of what have become known in hockey as "power forwards"—huge forwards who combine good skills and goal-scoring ability with an aggressive physical style and a willingness to fight. That combination of size, strength, skill, violence, and all-out effort has seen Shanahan post back-to-back 50-goal campaigns and be named a first-team All-Star in his nine-year NHL career. Add a healthy measure of intelligence and good humor and it's easy to understand why Shanahan has always found himself in a leadership role on and off the ice everywhere he's played. With London, his junior team in the OHL, in chaos, Shanahan, the 17-year-old captain, was left to run the squad's practices. He just missed the 40-goal mark in each of his two junior seasons, and was New Jersey's first choice, the second player taken overall, in the NHL's 1987 Entry Draft. Shanahan found the net only seven times in 65 games his rookie year while spending 131 minutes in the penalty box, but he established a physical presence that enabled him to improve his offensive contributions dramatically—50 points as a sophomore, 72 points in 1989-90. His numbers were almost identical in 1990-91—29 goals, 37 assists, and 141 penalty minutes—and when his contract expired he became one of the most avidly courted free agents in hockey. He wound up with St. Louis, setting off an involved and controversial compensation and arbitration process that eventually cost the Blues the services of All-Star defenseman Scott Stevens. It seemed an awfully high price to have to pay for the bruising left winger, who had put up respectable but unremarkable totals for the Devils. But Shanahan rammed home 33 goals in his first year in St. Louis and fought his way to 171 minutes in the sin bin, making him a huge fan favorite. They called him "Shan the Man." His reputation was enhanced by a series of TV promo spots he did for ESPN and other concerns, which revealed the film buff to be a natural actor as well as a witty, good-natured goofball. "He's our emotional leader," said his centerman, Craig Janney. Thanks to the generosity of the pass-happy Janney, Shanahan broke through with a big 51-goal season in 1992-93. Although not a fast or fluid skater, Shanahan's size, strength, and balance allow him to withstand a pounding when he plants himself near the opposition net waiting for a tip-in or rebound. In the open, his hard, accurate shot makes his patented one-timers lethal.

*I'M STILL STANDING-*
*Hartford's Brendan*
*Shanahan proves he's the*
*fittest in this confronta-*
*tion, leaving two Montreal play-*
*ers flat on the ice.*

"Brendan explodes in the attacking zone," commented Ron Caron, then the Blues' general manager. Shanahan did exactly that in '93-94. In a year of personal superlatives, Shanahan led the NHL with 397 shots on goal, and the barrage of rubber he launched paid off with production that earned him a berth on the NHL's First All-Star Team. He led the league with four hat tricks and seven short-handed goals, scored twice in the mid season All-Star game, and wound up topping even his marks of the previous season with 52 goals and 102 points in spite of spending 211 minutes in the cooler. Kevin Stevens, who had managed the feat two years earlier with Pittsburgh, is the

only other player ever to rack up 50 goals, 50 assists, and 100 points while taking 200 minutes in penalties.

In the final game of the regular season, Shanahan had his mouth ripped open and teeth knocked loose by the stick of Winnipeg's own superb power forward, Keith Tkachuk. Shanahan had the damage sewn up, and returned to the game to score two goals and pound Tkachuk to the ice. "There are just times in a game when somebody makes you mad and you want to do something dirty to them," Shanahan says. "There are times when I think the coach will forgive you for rolling your eyes back in your head and snapping—when he realizes it's an edge you can't take away. I don't condone foolish or stupid penalties, but I think there's a time and a place where you send a message."

"He's a pretty mean guy," acknowledges the Flyers' Eric Lindros, who knows whereof he speaks. "He can really flip."

Shanahan played briefly for Dusseldorf in the German League during the late-starting 1994-95 season, racking up eight points in only three games. German fans loved the affable, hulking North American, dubbing him "Shadherhan," after the towering cowboy action hero of popular German novels and films.

He returned to St. Louis to find Mike Keenan, fresh from leading the Rangers to the Stanley Cup, installed as coach and general manager, and his friend and linemate Janney traded away. Further hindered by a viral infection that caused his spleen to enlarge, Shanahan got off to a slow start and became the target of Keenan's wrath. "There are times every player needs a kick in the rear," Shanahan conceded, and he finished with 20 goals in 45 games, notching his 500th career point along the way. He fully returned to form with four goals and nine points before breaking his ankle in Game 5 of the Blues' opening-round playoff series against Vancouver. The Canucks wound up winning that game in overtime and taking the series in seven.

Keenan dealt Shanahan away that summer to Hartford for unproven young defenseman Chris Pronger, an emotional move for the St. Louis fans and for Shanahan. "I had four years

If he's not the top power forward in the league, he's right there in the top three. He's a younger Cam Neely.

to build memories there," Shanahan reflected, rattling off evocative moments like the 1993 playoff sweep of the Blackhawks. "To just totally demoralize guys like Chris Chelios, Ed Belfour and Jeremy Roenick felt good. That's a great memory."

If Blues fans were distraught, the Whalers were ecstatic. "If he's not the top power forward in the league, he's right there in the top three," declared Hartford general manager Jim Rutherford. "He's a younger Cam Neely."

Shanahan had the "C" sewn onto his sweater after just a week of training camp. "He's got tremendous leadership qualities," Holmgren observed. "They shone really from the first day he was here at his press conference. I think it's an ideal choice. I think the players in the room believe the same thing."

"It's an honor to be named captain of an NHL team," Shanahan said. "To come here on such short notice, and have that kind of faith put in me by management and my teammates, I hope I can do the job for them." He did, going on a midseason tear with 28 goals in 34 games. He finished with 44 on the year, and established himself as the centerpiece of Hartford's hopes for the future.

"Shanny just loves coming to work every day," says Jeff Brown, who's been Shanahan's teammate in both St. Louis and Hartford. "That doesn't mean he isn't a leader—he has always been a leader. He just approaches the game like a big kid—we all do, but he does a little more somehow. He is one of those guys who is going to play for a long, long time."

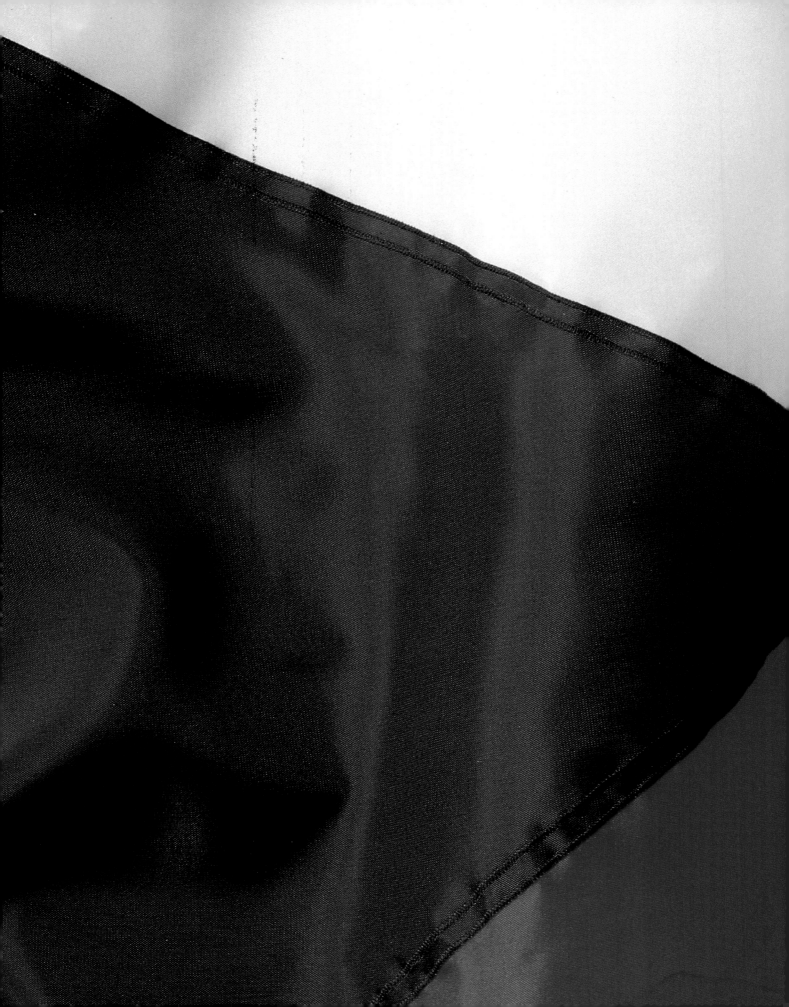

# Czech Republic and Slovakia

For many years, the Czechoslovakians have seemed close to world hockey's pinnacle without ever quite reaching it. They have certainly had their moments. In Prague in 1972, they won the World Championship, snapping the Soviets' nine-year run; they added further world crowns in '76 and '77; in '76, they came close to winning the Canada Cup, reaching the final only to have Darryl Sittler's overtime goal beat them. In '96 the Czech Republic gained some measure of revenge by beating Canada to win the World Championship. But far more often, they have had to settle for third, fourth, or fifth best.

But now that may be changing, even though Czechoslovakia has broken into two separate countries, the Czech Republic and Slovakia. In 1995, a young Czech named Jaromir Jagr became the first non-Canadian ever to win the Art Ross Trophy as the NHL's scoring leader. That same year, another Czech, Dominik Hasek, won his second consecutive Vezina Trophy as the NHL's premier goaltender. While so much attention has been paid to the influx of players from Scandinavia and the old Soviet Union, it just so happens that the best forward and best goalie in hockey are Czech.

1995 also marked the year that the NHL's leading goal-scorer, Peter Bondra, was a Slovak. And the following year, with Jagr, Hasek, and Bondra continuing to dominate, one of the season's biggest surprises was the emergence of two other young Slovaks, Zigmund Palffy and Petr Sykora, as NHL stars.

Maybe the surprise is not that Czechs and Slovaks have taken center stage, but that it has taken so long for it to happen. The history of hockey in Czechoslovakia extends back to the turn of the century, when the region was still known as Bohemia. It produced top-caliber teams in international play, and by the postwar era, Czechoslovakia was producing stars like Jozef Malecek and Vova Zabrodsky, who have since been compared to Gretzky and Beliveau.

In the wake of the Soviet invasion and occupation of 1968, Czechoslovak teams clashed with the USSR's national team in many incredibly tense and emotional confrontations. It was during this period that Vladimir Dzurilla shone. Considered the best goalie in European hockey in the '60s and an idol of Vladislav Tretiak, so great was he that he was coaxed out of a four-year retirement to compete in the 1976 Canada Cup. Sure enough, he led Czechoslovakia to a second-place finish and nearly stole them the tournament title.

They might have done it but for the absence of their big, high-scoring winger, Vaclav Nedomansky, who in 1974 had become the first eastern-bloc player to defect to the West. "Big Ned" was a potent goal-scorer in three WHA and six NHL seasons, and paved the way for a string of workmanlike older players the Czechoslovak hockey federation allowed to come to the NHL in the '70s and '80s.

But the greatest Czechoslovak star until now was still waiting in the wings. The Quebec Nordique-engineered cloak-and-dagger defection of Peter Stastny and his brother Anton, in the summer of 1980, was a cause célèbre. Once they had been whisked out from under the noses of their Czechoslovak minders at a tournament in Austria and brought to the NHL, they immediately made the Nordiques a force to be reckoned with. Joined the next season by brother Marian, they formed the only all-brother line in NHL history. Peter, as aggressive as he was prolific, achieved at exceptional levels; except for Wayne Gretzky, no other player scored as many points during the 1980s. On the international scene, Peter Stastny shifted his allegiance to Canada, but at the age of 37 he returned home to captain the new Slovak national team at the 1994 Lillehammer Olympics, distinguishing himself at that tournament.

Scores of Czechs and Slovaks have since graced the ice of NHL rinks, none more entertaining than the current generation, with Jagr, Hasek, Bondra, Palffy, Michal Pivonka, Radek Dvorak, Robert Svehla, and Roman Hamrlik. With players like these, and with those about to come over from the resurgent hockey powers of Central Europe, maybe their time is finally here.

# Roman Hamrlik

EVERY PARENT OF A TEENAGE BOY LEARNS THE VALUE OF PATIENCE. THE KID IS HEADSTRONG, OVER-confident, unpredictable; you can't talk to him, he listens to his friends instead of you; everything's cars, girls, and rock music. No matter how bright and talented he is, there's an inevitable amount of exasperation, recrimination, and worry; in the end, though, all you can really do is have faith that he'll find his way and turn out all right.    The Tampa Bay Lightning know exactly how it feels; they've played the role of nervous parent while Roman Hamrlik has gone through a difficult adolescence in the National Hockey League. But in the end, their faith has been rewarded. Just as they hoped, Hamrlik has emerged as one of hockey's top defensemen.    Hamrlik entered the league with the honor—and pressure—of being the first choice overall in the 1992 draft, the first player ever selected by the expansion Lightning, the player around whom the future of the franchise would be built. The strapping 18-year-old native of Gottwaldov, Czechoslovakia, had drawn the attention of NHL scouts with strong showings at the 1991 and 1992 World Junior Championships.    "I don't mind pressure," said Hamrlik when he was drafted. "I just like to play my game and work to be the best." But Hamrlik's capabilities seemed at first to fall far short of the hype surrounding him. A season and a half in the Czechoslovak Elite League had not prepared the teenager for the pace of NHL play. He spoke almost no English, making instruction in practice, let alone communication during games, difficult; he became better known around the league for his defensive-zone gaffes and passion for heavy metal and sports cars than for his on-ice performance.    "The language was the toughest part," Hamrlik recalls. "There was no one to talk to, except for family. It was hard." Lightning general manager Phil Esposito made it easier, acquiring Petr Klima, the Czech veteran of seven NHL campaigns. "He's been like a brother," says Hamrlik. "We do things away from ice, like fish, play tennis, go to dinner. And on ice, he explains everything so that I can understand. I really didn't start understanding anything until he came here."    Hamrlik's rookie numbers were disappointing, and although he played aggressively and showed flashes of skill, the youngster seemed out of sync throughout his sophomore season as well. The big teen was at odds with himself, trying to blend his penchant for board-rattling hits with his admiration for the graceful rushing style of his long-time idol, Bruin superstar

Ray Bourque. He also had to reconcile the instructions of his Tampa Bay coaches with the often contradictory advice of his father, an amateur coach in Czechoslovakia who had moved to the States with his family to be with Roman and brother Martin, a prospect in the Hartford system.

Hamrlik's career hit its low point in April 1994 when he tore knee ligaments playing for the Czech Republic in a World Championship pretournament game. Tampa Bay's director of hockey operations, Tony Esposito, defended the decision to allow the foundation of the franchise to compete in non-NHL action: "Our feeling is, if a guy wants to play for his country, he should be allowed to play. Roman really wanted to play. And really, we thought the experience would be good for Roman. It's just one of those things."

The rigorous rehabilitation of his damaged knee produced a more focused, mature player. Hamrlik's skills began to jell in 1995, and he emerged as a leader on the ice. "He has been carrying us lately, there's no doubt about that," said Lightning coach Terry Crisp. Added assistant coach Wayne Cashman: "We're starting to use him more and more. In every situation, power play, penalty killing, he's the guy we're going to. He wanted the extra pressure, the responsibility. It's like he thrives on it."

"I want to be on the ice," assented Hamrlik. "I want them to count on me. I can handle it."

Hamrlik finished third in goal-scoring among NHL defensemen in '95, and was

He's doing the kind of things a Bourque does now—the way he controls a game and works at both ends of the ice.

rewarded with a lucrative four-year contract. "Adjusting to the NHL was hard," Hamrlik admits. "Lots of tough times. But I get better, more relaxed, more sure of myself. Now I try to play more my style of game. Lots of hits and I hope lots of goals." Hamrlik smiles as the skull-shattering strains of Metallica blare from his boom-box in the Lightning dressing room. "It has to be hard, go fast. . . . That's the way I play—hard, fast, like my music."

That's how Hamrlik played in his fourth NHL season. He took smarter chances in the opposition end and cut down on mistakes in his own end, still dealing out heavy hits while using his strong skating, crisp passing, and a quick, hard shot to produce at nearly a point-a-game pace. His performance earned him a berth alongside Bourque on the Eastern Conference team at the 1996 All-Star Game—even if it did mean he had to miss an AC/DC concert in Tampa.

"I was really looking forward to seeing AC/DC," Hamrlik said. "Could have had back-stage pass and everything. But this is much better. I go to All-Star Game instead, because this is dream come true. That will be one of best things about All-Star Game—get to play with Ray Bourque. Wow! That will be awesome."

Bourque himself says, "When you talk about stars in this league, I think he's already there. I've watched him, and he has all the tools. He could be a regular at the All-Star Game for many years to come."

*GETTING TO KNOW YOU- Tampa Bay's Roman Hamrlik introduces himself to Chicago's Jeremy Roenick along the boards.*

*MISSION IMPOSSIBLE-*
*Tampa Bay's Roman*
*Hamrlik has the unenviable*
*task of trying to knock*
*Philadelphia's Eric Lindros*
*off the puck.*

# Dominik Hasek

MEET DOMINIK HASEK ON THE STREET—WIRY, ANGULAR, SOFT-SPOKEN, A LITTLE NERVOUS—and you might take him for an accountant or librarian, not a hockey player. But a hockey player he is, and not just any player at that. 🏒 Right now, Hasek just happens to be one of the best goaltenders on earth. In fact, he has been for the last few years, but people have only started realizing it lately. Maybe it's his appearance and demeanor that delayed him recognition in North America. Perhaps it's the peculiar lack of success that other European goalies, with the exception of the late Pelle Lindbergh, have enjoyed in NHL play. Most likely, it's Hasek's own style in the nets, which is certainly unique and could even be called bizarre. 🏒 Hasek flops and sprawls and flails like an octopus on the ice; he sprints out to the blue line to thwart breakaways; he throws away his stick to pounce on loose pucks near the goal crease; he spins and rolls to stop shots with his back to the shooter. He's been described as "a break-dancing Gumby" between the pipes. Hasek was born to play goal, but his style is one he's bred himself. 🏒 "Ever since I can remember, I always made straight for the goal—in soccer, in hockey, in everything," Hasek says, recalling the evolution of his *sui generis* play. "When I was ten or eleven, I'd go and watch the practice of the junior team—and I'd just pay attention to what the goalie was doing and think about it. And then I'd try it all out in my practices. Sometimes it was a matter of rotating my inside foot a few degrees to set up a different rebound, to make the puck bounce farther away. Coaches never told me anything . . . except keep my stick on the ice." 🏒 Hasek, the son of a uranium miner, got his break early. Jiri Crha, the star goaltender for Tesla Pardubice, the powerful Czechoslovak Elite League team in Hasek's hometown, defected for a shot in the NHL. At the age of 16, Hasek was called up to replace him. 🏒 Hasek quickly became a superstar, the finest goaltender in his nation since Olympic hero Vladimir Dzurilla, maybe the best ever. He was named MVP of the 1983 World Junior Championships. He was hailed as Czechoslovak goalie of the year five times in a row and player of the year three straight times. Twice he earned best-goalie honors at the World Championships. 🏒 "I always secretly hoped that I'd come to the NHL, even when I was still a kid in Pardubice," says Hasek, "because in hockey, it's not the Olympics where it's at, or the World Championship, it's the NHL." Nevertheless, he turned down a Blackhawks contract offer in 1987 because it meant he would have to defect and leave his family behind the Iron Curtain. Plus, he adds, "I wanted to finish the university. I always thought I'd wind up teaching history at some high school when I quit hockey." 🏒

*THE TERMINATOR-When the Dominator is between the pipes, nothing gets past him.*

Hasek continued to star in Czechoslovakia until the communist regime suddenly evaporated, and he was free to test his skills in North America. He signed with the Blackhawks in 1990 and performed well in a handful of appearances. But with all-star Ed Belfour ensconced as starter and a raft of prospects ahead of him awaiting their turn in the barrel, Hasek found himself consigned to the minors, although he excelled there as well, a First Team IHL All-Star.

Hasek's self-taught style inspired little faith in NHL coaches who adhered to the orthodoxy of stand up. "He flops around the ice like some fish," sneered a Blackhawks' assistant. It took a trade to Buffalo in the summer of 1992 before Hasek finally got a real chance in the NHL, and his game rose to extraordinary levels once he was finally assured of the starting job in 1993–94. He seemed unbeatable, and every save seemed spectacular, leaving shooters around the league shaking their heads in disbelief. Here was a goaltender whose play was as exciting to watch as that of the flashiest playmakers and goal-scorers in the NHL. At the end of the year, Hasek's incredible statistics were a perfect reflection of his jaw-dropping on-ice performances. He led the NHL with an inconceivable .930 save percentage and 1.95 goals-against average. Hasek was not only the first European ever to lead NHL goalkeepers in goals-against, he was the first NHL goalie in 20 years, since the great Bernie Parent, to allow less than two goals a game.

"Boy, to have a season under two goals a game, that's just impossible in this day and age," noted John Davidson, former star netminder of the Rangers. "And I don't see any Bobby Orrs or Serge Savards playing defense in front of him." The Sabres averaged barely three goals a game in Hasek's starts, yet he earned the win in 30 of them. And he didn't even mind the lack of support. "It's very important that I feel people like me here," he explained. "It's why I play so well, because the players, coaches, the people in the stadium, believe in me."

Hasek's brilliance reached an apotheosis against the New Jersey Devils in the opening round of the 1994 Stanley Cup playoffs. He and the Devils' Martin Brodeur battled all through Game 6, each stopping every one of the 31 shots through three periods, then again through one full overtime, and again through another, and then, unimaginably, through a third. Both goalies had posted the equivalent of two full back-to-back shutouts in one night, and while the Devils' rookie was unshakably steady, Hasek became increasingly spectacular, blocking 39 more shots in sudden-death overtime, Brodeur just 19, before Buffalo scored 5:43 into the fourth overtime period. It was only the second NHL playoff game since 1943 to extend to four overtimes, and the Dominator had stopped 70 shots for the shutout. New Jersey went on to a narrow Game 7 win, but Hasek finished with a .950 save percentage, capping a sensational Vezina Trophy regular season with a fantastic playoff performance.

He continued to stand on his head in 1995,

It's not just a case of Dominik being the most valuable player for the Sabres. He's probably the most valuable player in the NHL.

duplicating his astronomical .930 save percentage, again leading the league, and winning his second straight Vezina. "I don't think it's just a case of Dominik being the most valuable player for the Buffalo Sabres," said John Muckler, the Sabres general manager. "He's probably the most valuable player in the NHL right now. I can't begin to imagine where we would be without him."

Muckler concedes that Hasek's style "goes against all the principles of goaltending, but he always knows what he's doing. He's a thinking goaltender." Adds Davidson: "Dominik has great athletic ability, an elastic body, maybe the quickest legs in the game, and he's a master of doing the unexpected. I think it took this long for him to get a real shot because of his eccentricity. But these days there's more of a hands-off attitude: If they stop the puck, who cares how they do it?"

"What's good for one goalie isn't good for another," says Hasek. "It's my style. I never think about it. I always believe that every goal you give up, you could have done something different to stop it. I always wonder what I could do better. If I do a butterfly, I tell myself I probably should have stood up."

Hasek has few occasions to second-guess himself. Although the team in front of him was, to put it mildly, in the midst of a rebuilding year, he was the league's leading goaltender again in 1995–96.

"I think you have to look at him and think of the Hart Trophy," says Muckler. "He's not just a great goaltender, he's one of the great players. He's an amazing athlete."

# Jaromir Jagr

"YOU ALWAYS WANT TO SCORE THE BEAUTIFUL GOAL."  IT'S THE ABILITY TO SAY THAT, AS WELL AS TO DO it, that makes Jaromir Jagr such a breath of fresh air. One of the unfortunate facts about North American athletes is that they rarely talk about the beauty of the game or the joy of playing it—all too often they reduce their marvelous exploits to a bland "just doing my job." But not Jagr. Not only does the Pittsburgh Penguins' shaggy-maned teen idol from the Czech Republic make breathtaking plays and plenty of them, he *likes* doing it, and he isn't afraid to say so. "I just go out and have fun," he says. "If you have fun, I think you play a lot better than if you take the game seriously." A lot of coaches might cringe at that statement, but none can argue with the results: In his first six NHL seasons, the right winger had already accumulated over 220 goals and 315 assists, a points-per-game average that had risen every year (from .71 in 1991 to 1.82 in 1996), one league scoring title, two Stanley Cups, recognition for having tallied one of the most amazing goals in the history of the game, and, last but not least, a following that made him one of Pittsburgh's most beloved athletes, of any sport, in any era. Big, fast, virtually impossible to knock off his feet (even though everyone tries), Jagr is the kind of guy who skates around and through both defensemen, fakes the goalie out of his pads, deposits the puck in the net—then blows kisses to the wildly cheering crowd. Jagr was always something of a rebel. He was born in Kladno, Czechoslovakia, in 1972—four years after Soviet tanks rolled into the country to crush the brief flowering of free expression and liberalism known as the Prague Spring. Growing up with his mother and father on his grandmother's farm just outside town, his grandmother told him stories about her late husband—how he lost most of the farm to collectivization when the communists came to power in 1948; how he was jailed in 1966 for defying the government; how he died in prison in 1968, not long before the Soviet invasion. By the time Jagr was 12 he'd come to disbelieve most of what he'd been taught in school about politics, so he stuck a picture of Ronald Reagan, the fiercely anticommunist U.S. president who'd called the Soviet Union an "evil empire," in his notebook and carried it with him to class every day. When Jagr was six, his father enrolled him in a league for six-year-olds, another for eight-year-olds, and still another for 10-year-olds, so that he could get plenty of action, mainly against much older boys. By the time Jagr became a teenager, he had heard a little bit about Wayne Gretzky and seen Mario Lemieux play at the 1985 World Championships in Prague. "Those were the only names I knew," says Jagr. "But I knew about life in America, and I

*FLIRTING WITH DISAS-TER-Any time Pittsburgh's Jaromir Jagr is this close to the net, it could spell disaster for the opposing team.*

knew about the NHL. My first goal was always to play for the local team in my city. My second goal was to play for the national team of Czechoslovakia, because that is my country. But my third goal was to play in the NHL, because that is the best hockey in the world."

Jagr realized those goals in a hurry. He debuted on the Poldi Kladno team at 16. His second year there, 1989–90, was an eventful one. It started

with the Velvet Revolution, when Czechoslovakia threw off communism and the Soviet occupiers without the loss of a single life. On the ice, young Jagr led his club in scoring and shone with both the national junior and senior teams. That June he became the first Czechoslovak player ever to attend the NHL draft without defecting—thus avoiding the quandary faced by so many other athletes of his nationality, like his idol Martina

Navratilova, whose poster occupied a spot next to Wayne Gretzky's in his boyhood bedroom.

Pittsburgh chose Jagr in the first round, fifth overall. The rest, as they say, is history. He chose to wear No. 68 with the Penguins to honor his homeland and his grandfather. In his rookie year he overcame homesickness and language problems to score a promising 57 regular-season points. With his stickhandling talent, 6-2, 208-pound physique, and uniform number in the 60s, people couldn't help but notice Jagr's resemblance to Lemieux. Even his first name, *Jaromir*, is an anagram for *Mario Jr.* In the playoffs, Mario Jr. added 13 postseason points—including an overtime game-winner in the opening round—en route to the Penguins' first-ever Stanley Cup.

In '91–92 he improved to 69 regular-season points and 24 playoff points, but what was really impressive was the way he stepped up to lead the Pens when Lemieux suffered a broken hand in the quarterfinals against New York. Jagr broke open Game 5 with a penalty-shot goal and, late in the third period, a game-winning solo effort in which he left a trail of sprawling Rangers in his wake. The 20-year-old notched the series winner in the next game, but his masterpiece came in Game 1 of the Cup Final against Chicago. With Pittsburgh trailing by one with five minutes to go, Jagr took the puck in the Blackhawk zone, eluded a check, then weaved through three more Blackhawks before faking goalie Ed Belfour out of position and driving the biscuit home. That goal, which many hockey people—including Lemieux himself—call the greatest they've ever seen, set the stage for the eventual sweep that gave the Pens their second straight Cup.

Jaromir would head to the video game, and there'd be a hundred 17- and 18-year-old girls giving him quarters.

The next two years, Jagr tempered the disappointment of early-round playoff exits—and the peaceful breakup of his native land into two distinct nations, Slovakia and his own Czech Republic—by coping with the Jagrmania that gripped his adopted city. "We'd go out and he'd head to the video game," recalls ex-teammate Rick Tocchet, "and there'd be a hundred 17- and 18-year-old girls lined up behind him, giving him quarters."

Then came his fabulous '95 campaign. With the recuperating Lemieux sitting out the shortened season, Jagr became the first European-trained player ever to win the NHL scoring crown, and the first noncenter to win it since Guy Lafleur in 1978. In '95–96, Jagr picked up where he left off, waging a friendly season-long battle with the rejuvenated Lemieux for another scoring title (and breaking Peter Stastny's 14-year-old record for single-season scoring by a European in the process). He just kept getting better, just kept having more fun, whether steaming in on goal solo—"I've seen him skate with [225-pound Ranger defenseman Jeff] Beukeboom on his back," said a teammate, "and it was like he was skating with an extra sweater"—or helping his linemates, countryman Petr Nedved and the great center Ron Francis, to best-ever seasons.

"I've always loved hockey," says Jagr. "But I've never loved it this much." Those are ominous words for the Pens' NHL opponents and the Czech Republic's international foes. But for everyone else, it's a promise of countless new thrills to come.

# Peter Bondra

YOU CAN ALWAYS SPOT A GREAT GOAL-SCORER FROM THE WAY HE CELEBRATES HIS GOALS. WHEN THE average player puts the puck in the net, his reaction, usually, is understated; he may raise his arms, but the expression on his face is muted, even sullen, as though he doesn't want to be seen even presuming to celebrate. Not so the sniper. No matter how many hundreds of goals he has scored, he jubilates as if it's his first. Think of the great target men of recent times, and how they'd react when they lit the lamp. Esposito's broad look of delight as he happily bear hugged his Bruin teammates. Lafleur's winning grin as he skated past, his long hair trailing in the breeze. Gretzky's boyish smile, as though the goal were a rarity instead of something he'd done hundreds upon hundreds of times before in his career. And you could say the same of Bossy, Lemieux, Messier, the Hulls—father and son—and so many other goal-scoring greats, all expressing the joy and release of achieving what every skater ultimately strives for: the goal. That's how you could tell Peter Bondra was headed for greatness, even several years ago, when he was just another young import trying to prove he belonged in the NHL. Bondra scored 40 goals in his first 125 regular-season games—a healthy total, but hardly an indication that he would soon blossom into one of hockey's deadliest shooters. But even then, Bondra could celebrate. He'd jump up and down, pump his arms, scream with joy, leap against the glass. He was one-man pandemonium, except that all the Washington Capitals' fans in the building would be celebrating with him. "Every goal I score," says the 6-1, 200-pound Slovak, "I'm happy. Even when my teammates score and I don't, I'm happy. That's why I'm playing, playing for goals and victory. Some keep [emotions] inside. I just put them outside. People seem to like it, that's OK too." People are getting more and more chances to see whether they like it, because Bondra is beating goalies more and more often. In the abbreviated 1995 season, the Caps' left-shooting right wing led the league with 34 goals in 47 games—a total surpassed in an NHL season of that length only by the legendary Charlie Conacher's 36 in 1934-35. A contract dispute kept Bondra out of the first six games of '95-96, but that didn't stop him from potting 52 goals in 67 games, good for fourth in the league in that category. One of the secrets to Bondra's success, the thing that enables him to consummate his hunger for goals, is his explosive acceleration, which enables him to burst free of his check and into the open, with or without the puck. "I've seen some fast guys," says his long-time Capitals centerman, Michal Pivonka, "but when he gets going he's one of the fastest in the league. The first couple years he had the speed, but didn't know how to use it. Now he's learning how to drive to the net or go wide when that's smart." Adds teammate Dale Hunter: "His speed is the thing. He's flat-out burning people now."

Bondra was born in Ukraine in 1968, but moved with his family to Czechoslovakia at age three. There he grew up playing the game, and reached the Czechoslovak Elite League in 1986-87 with Kosice. In his last two years with the club, he put up the kind of goal-heavy scoring totals that would become his statistical trademark on these shores: 30 goals and 10 assists in 40 games in 1988-89, 36 goals and 19 assists in 49 games in 1989-90.

Drafted by Washington in the eighth round of the 1990 draft, Bondra came directly to the Capitals without spending a moment in the minor leagues. Despite having to acclimate himself to the rougher North American style as well as to a new language and culture, Bondra did well enough his first two years to keep a regular spot with the Caps.

In '92-93 he broke through with a 37-goal, 48-assist season that earned him his first invitation to the midseason All-Star Game. "He made a commitment to pay the price," said Caps coach Jim Schoenfeld. "He became a consistent player once he decided he wanted to be a consistent player." He crowned his year by helping Slovakia win the Olympic qualifying tournament in its first appearance as an independent nation.

But the following NHL season, Bondra dropped off to just 24 goals (despite a five-goal game against Tampa Bay that included a league-record four markers in a 4:12 stretch), saddling him

E very goal I
score, I'm happy.
That's why I'm
playing, playing
for goals
and victory.

with a reputation as an inconsistent, streaky player. That didn't sit well with Bondra, so he resolved to do something about it. "Bondra, typical of Europeans, came over as an excellent skater not used to the physical game," said Caps strength and conditioning coach Frank Costello. "He did not have a strong upper body." That summer, Bondra added nine pounds of upper-body muscle. When training camp opened the ensuing September, remembered Costello, "As soon as he walked in the door, I said, 'Hey, he did his homework.'"

"I worked in the off-season and during the labor dispute to build my upper-body strength," said Bondra, "not that I could kill someone, but so that when someone hit me I could take the hit without falling down."

The plan worked. Although the new, fortified Bondra started tentatively, he gained steam as the shortened season proceeded, bulling through checks and enduring goalmouth punishment to notch 23 tallies in his final 21 contests. Those are impressive numbers in any year, but considering that 1995 was the year of the offense-smothering neutral-zone trap, Bondra's numbers were fantastic.

Most of Bondra's goals were assisted by Pivonka, from the Czech Republic. Together they also spearheaded the dogged checking that has long been a Caps' staple. "He kills penalties with me now," said Pivonka. "No question about it, he's improved." True enough—Bondra's six short-handed goals also led the NHL in '95.

When both Bondra and Pivonka returned from their brief holdout at the start of '95-96, they had to prove the previous season was no fluke. They

did. "When you have a player like Bondra who has as much speed as he has," said Rangers goalie Glenn Healy, "he creates havoc for the defense, which in turn would create havoc for the goaltender."

That was exactly the formula Bondra used to record another fabulous season and cement his reputation as one of the most productive and exciting scorers in hockey today—and to perform more of his memorable goal-celebration dances.

"I don't know why he does those things," says a bemused Pivonka. "I've seen some guys do things like that—not on this level—but Peter, I don't know what he's doing."

To which the smiling Slovak can only reply, "I'm happy with myself because I scored a goal." Naturally. Great goal-scorers always are.

*BREAKING AWAY-Washington's Peter Bondra breaks away from the pack en route to the net.*

*EXECUTIVE DECISION-Washington's Peter Bondra has a lot on his mind—like what is the most direct route to the net.*

# Russia

They seemed to come from nowhere, these red-clad snipers, swooping across the ice, making impossible passes, flaunting their mastery of a game Canadians had thought was theirs alone. Their circling, constant-motion game dazzled and confused a lane-bound North American style that had grown complacent in its isolation. But here it was, 1972, the first game of the Summit Series, and the Soviets had stunned the NHL's best in Montreal, 7-3. Today, most North Americans, when they talk about the '72 series, speak of Paul Henderson's series-winning goal in Moscow. But the real meaning of that series was that the unheralded Soviets were every bit the equal of the very best Canada could summon. And from there, the Soviets would only get better.

The Cold War had left many in the West ignorant of the degree to which hockey had developed, or even that it had been developing, behind the Iron Curtain. But in fact, Russians had been playing a form of hockey—bandy—since the late 19th century. Bandy, still popular throughout Scandinavia and Russia, consists of 11 players a side playing with field hockey sticks and a small ball, on a sheet of ice the size of a soccer pitch.

On February 17, 1946, a crowd of several thousand attended a bandy match played by students from the Moscow Institute of Physical Culture, then stayed as primitive boards were set up to form a rink of Canadian dimensions, and witnessed the first Soviet exhibition of Canadian-style hockey. The game was a hit with everyone present, and that fall, many of the USSR's leading soccer clubs embarked on a hockey season. Hockey in Russia was born.

The Soviet Union would have no indoor rinks until 1956, so games were staged outside in the bone-cracking chill of Russian winter nights. A rink was set up at one end of the enormous Dinamo soccer stadium in Moscow, drawing crowds of 30,000, still the largest ever to see a hockey game anywhere. "Oh, those hockey vigils on the east tribune of Dinamo under the soundless, implacable tramping of thousands of boots!" the newspaper *Komsomolskaya Pravda* later recalled. "No frost could stop the movement on the floodlit rink, surrounded by snowdrifts, where athletes wearing biking helmets, since we had no hockey helmets at the time, created a game."

No helmets, no sticks, no artificial ice, but they turned that very lack of equipment to their advantage. Their famous land training methods were necessitated by lack of ice, their accurate wrist shots came from their fear of breaking precious sticks on slap shots. Even their uniforms were raggedy; anyone who saw that '72 series noticed how the thread that attached numbers to sweaters often unraveled over the course of the games. The architect of the transition from the 11-man to the six-man game was Anatoli Tarasov. Harnessing the skills of Soviet national soccer team superstar Vsevelod Bobrov, as spectacular a scorer on ice as on grass, Tarasov coached the Soviet team to victory in their first world tournament, in Stockholm in 1954. In 24 years at the helm of the national team (1948-72), Tarasov claimed an incredible nine world titles, plus another 18 Soviet League crowns with CSKA.

The Soviets' unassailable domination of international hockey in the '60s at last led to the dramatic confrontation of the 1972 Summit Series. It was there that North American fans first came to know the names of thrilling forwards like Mikhailov, Kharlamov, Petrov, Yakushev, Maltsev, and Shadrin, and that of their incomparable goalie Vladislav Tretiak. The Soviets responded to the rugged, sometimes bullying tactics of many NHL teams by simply turning the other cheek. They proceeded to reel off an impressive array of victories on North American ice: in 1974 against a WHA-based Team Canada, in the 1979 Challenge Cup against the NHL all-stars, in the 1981 Canada Cup, trouncing Canada 8-1 in the final game, and in the 1988 Calgary Olympics. Through the '70s and '80s club teams like CSKA (also known as Central Army or by the misnomer Central Red Army), Dinamo Moscow, Wings of the Soviet, and Spartak Moscow toured NHL cities, regularly drubbing their opponents.

Ultimately, the Soviet national team was both a product and a reflection of the Soviet political system. The discipline that controlled players' movement on the ice extended to control of players' off-ice activities as well. Cracks in the unified facade began to show in the late '80s, when the great defenseman Viacheslav Fetisov spoke out and promising young forward Alexander Mogilny defected. As the communist system in the Soviet Union began to break down, so did the Big Red Machine of Soviet hockey. Finally, in 1989, the hockey authorities allowed some stars to play in the NHL—Fetisov, his defense partner Alexei Kasatonov, and the KLM linemates Krutov, Larionov, and Makarov. A year later, young stars like Sergei Fedorov and Pavel Bure arrived.

Today, almost every NHL team boasts a Soviet-trained player on its roster. And the Russian style of hockey, once derided by Cold War-era North Americans as "robotic" and "soulless," is now recognized for what it always was: creative, artistic, courageous, and wildly entertaining.

# Pavel Bure

THE LAUNCH OF THE ROCKET WAS ABORTED ALMOST ON TAKEOFF IN 1995. THAT'S THE RUSSIAN ROCKET, better known as Pavel Bure of the Vancouver Canucks, and it wasn't only Vancouver fans who were disappointed. The loss of Bure to a severe knee injury in November deprived hockey fans everywhere of the opportunity to react with "oohs" and "ahhs" to some of the most spectacular offensive fireworks in the game. 🏒 "I've played with and against a lot of great players," says former Canucks coach Rick Ley. "But I've never seen a player like him where you stand behind the bench, watch him, and just say 'wow.'" Coaches, teammates, opponents, and fans alike have been saying just that since Bure was a kid growing up in Moscow. His eye-popping acceleration, speed, and maneuverability put fans in the stands, and every time he touches the puck he puts them on the edge of their seats. 🏒 As a boy, Bure's favorite players were Boris Mikhailov and fast and flashy Valeri Kharlamov, two of the greatest stars of the superb Central Army and Soviet national teams of the 1970s. "It was every kid's dream to play for the Army team," remembers Bure. "When I was 17, I made it to the Army team and accomplished my dream." 🏒 In 1988-89, Bure earned Soviet Elite League rookie-of-the-year honors with CSKA, then was named the World Junior Tournament's outstanding forward as the Soviet juniors romped to the gold medal. 🏒 Bure skated with two other immensely talented youngsters who would also go on to NHL stardom, Sergei Fedorov and Alexander Mogilny. The trio was intended to succeed the fabled KLM line of Vladimir Krutov, Igor Larionov, and Sergei Makarov, who had performed brilliantly for the Soviets for a decade. But Mogilny defected to North America in 1989, and Fedorov a year later. Bure remained a vital member of the Soviet junior and national teams, both of which won gold in 1990. Still only 19, he rifled in 35 goals in 44 league games in 1990-91. 🏒 But he was disturbed by the conditions of the contract presented him by CSKA. So Bure, along with his father Vladimir, a three-time medalist as an Olympic swimmer, and his younger brother Valeri, now a regular for the Montreal Canadiens, slipped off to Los Angeles. Quickly signing with a player agent and arranging a sham green-card marriage with an American model known as "Jymi," Bure was ensconced in North America and ready to sign with the Canucks, who had drafted him in '89. 🏒 He lost little time making an impact in the NHL. He racked up 34 goals in 65 games, then added 10 points in 13 postseason games, leading the Canucks to their first playoff series win in 10 long years. Bure was awarded the Calder Trophy as the NHL's best rookie. 🏒 He followed up with a sensational 60-goal,

50-assist sophomore season, rolling up 12 points in 12 playoff games as Vancouver again got past the first round but no further. By now, Bure was practically being worshiped in Vancouver, beloved as much for his boyish good looks as for his on-ice heroics.

Intensely private and extremely reticent, Bure admitted to a justifiable confidence in his talents. "I don't want to say I will score every game," he said. "But I think it is possible."

Indeed, he came close again in 1993-94, with a second straight 60-goal campaign and another 107 points. Bure's hundredth career goal came in his 154th NHL game, making him the sixth-fastest ever to reach the milestone, after Mike Bossy, Maurice Richard (the original Rocket), Joe Nieuwendyk, Wayne Gretzky, and Teemu Selanne. The right winger's 60 goals led the league and earned him a spot on the NHL First All-Star Team, the first Canuck ever to achieve either distinction. He was at his hottest down the stretch—49 of his goals came in the season's last 50 games.

Vancouver faced Calgary in the opening round of the 1994 playoffs and fell behind 3-1 in games. An overtime win staved off elimination, and two nights later Bure assisted on Trevor Linden's overtime winner. Game 7 was back in Calgary. The Flames took an early lead, but a Bure goal tied it in the first period. Trailing again with less than four minutes left, Bure set up a Greg Adams goal that sent the game into sudden death. After one excruciating overtime period and two minutes of a second, Bure flashed into the open and snapped home the winner. "The best goal I have ever scored," Bure called it.

I've played with and against a lot of great players. But I've never seen a player like him.

He remained in the spotlight in the quarter-finals, and not just for his scoring. Physically pummeled by Dallas checking, which he felt crossed the line into unpenalized thuggery, Bure took a run from behind at Stars' knuckle man Shane Churla, knocking him out with an elbow to the head. The infraction went unseen. Bure got off with a small fine and had no regrets. "Why should I be suspended if they're not suspended?" he asked. "I got a couple of real good crosschecks from behind, and if the referees don't call it I have to protect myself. It's not my style of play, but I had no choice."

A relatively small 5-10 and 187, Bure's production doesn't suffer much in a physical game. "Pavel gets better the more you hit him," says Gino Odjick, Vancouver's resident tough guy and Bure's best friend on the team.

The Canucks reached the Stanley Cup Final against the New York Rangers, and again came from a 3 games to 1 deficit to tie the series. They finally succumbed to the Ranger team of destiny, but Bure had carried the Canucks further than anyone expected, leading all playoff goal scorers with 16 and amassing 31 points in 24 postseason games.

1995 was a letdown in Vancouver, but during the summer, the Canucks acquired Bure's supersonic old linemate Mogilny, and the 1995-96 campaign became something to dream about.

"You can visualize what it will be like seeing them playing together, and that prospect is very exciting," said Canucks general manager Pat Quinn. "But we also know when it comes time to getting them on the ice, things don't always go as planned." He couldn't know how prophetic that was.

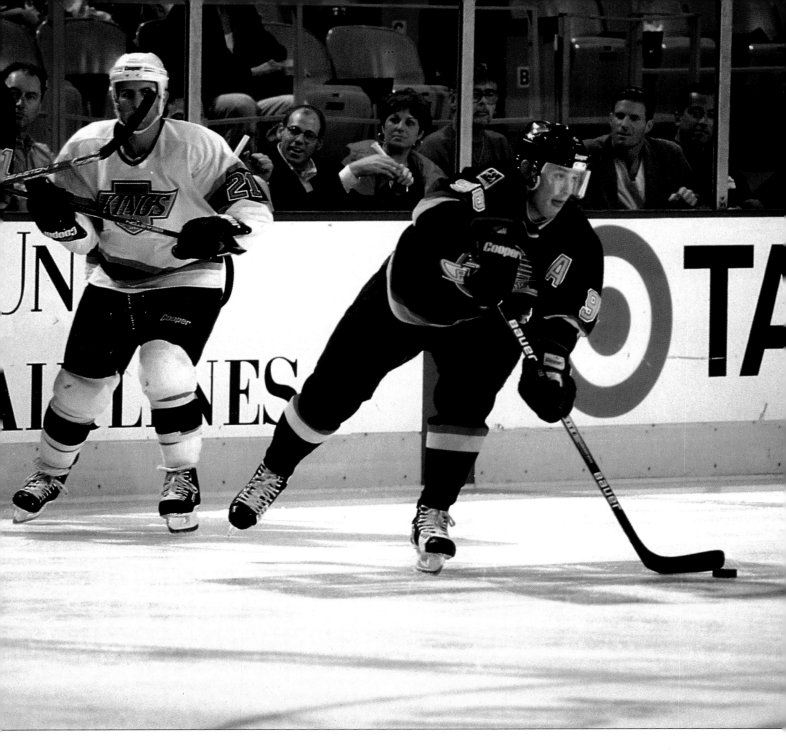

The pair started slowly before clicking to combine for 12 points in three November games. It seemed the old magic had been rekindled when Bure suddenly went down for the season with a torn ligament in his right knee.

Alone, Mogilny still had a great year, but without the Russian Rocket, the Canucks went out in the playoffs' opening round. That summer, however, his rehab was nearly complete, and fans in North America's Most Beautiful City looked forward to a season in which, they hoped, Bure would answer their Stanley Cup prayers.

Why not? After all, says former teammate Geoff Courtnall. "He's God in Vancouver."

*INDEPENDENCE DAY-The Russian Rocket Pavel Bure is free to do as he pleases, as he picks up the puck in the open ice.*

# Sergei Fedorov

PUT A HIGH-SCORING NATURAL CENTER ON THE WING. CUT HIS ICE TIME BY A THIRD. QUESTION HIS EFFORT when he's injured. Even have him play a few games back on defense. How do you think he'll respond—by sulking? Slacking off? Disappearing from the scoring summaries? If he's Sergei Fedorov of the Detroit Red Wings, he'll just take it in stride and give you another hundred-point season. ⬤ "For a true hockey person—not someone who finds excitement out of the game or exhilaration from the speed, but for someone who understands—he's an artisan who does spectacular things to boot," says David Conte, New Jersey's assistant director of scouting. ⬤ At 26, Fedorov has already been named the NHL's most valuable player, its best defensive forward, contended for the league scoring title, and proven himself the fastest skater in hockey. For all the quiet pride he may take in those achievements, though, he'd trade them all for the most important reward that has remained out of reach. "The goals don't mean anything to me now. It doesn't matter who scores now, as long as someone does," he said during the 1996 playoffs. "I want to win the Stanley Cup. Isn't that what this is all about?" ⬤ The 6-1, 200-pound Fedorov is a native of Pskov, a Russian city just south of Finland on the Estonian border. "Every year when I was a kid," he says, recalling a dreamlike tableau, "we skated on a river and there was a plant that would freeze in the middle of the water. It was a green plant with a white flower. I can still see it . . . part of it would stick up above the ice. We used to skate around this plant, looking at it. It was good exercise." ⬤ Encouraged by his father Viktor, a former league soccer player, Fedorov, like so many Canadian players who were "river skaters" as kids, developed astonishing speed, grace, and stamina. "Training secret—," he confides, "my father told me the first five steps are the most important." ⬤ Great skating was a prerequisite for players on the great Soviet Central Army and national teams. Fedorov, who grew up idolizing Soviet legends Sergei Makarov, Igor Larionov, and Slava Fetisov, found himself, at age 16, playing with them for CSKA. "You don't know what that gave to me," Fedorov says. "It was big for my development. Those four years made me from teenager to professional hockey player. It gave me my base." He still retains the Soviet land-training regimen—running, cycling, and so on—to maintain his terrific conditioning. ⬤ Highlights of Fedorov's Soviet career include his six goals and 12 points in seven games at the 1988 World Junior Championships, helping his country to the silver medal, and being part of the Soviet team that won gold at both the 1989 and 1990 World Championships. He also served as pivot on the sensational young line

*IT'S A BIRD, IT'S A PLANE, IT'S SERGEI FEDOROV-Detroit's Sergei Fedorov is able to leap hockey sticks in a single bound.*

that featured Pavel Bure and Alexander Mogilny on the wings.

But Soviet hockey's hope for the future eroded as Mogilny, Fedorov, and Bure defected in successive seasons. Fedorov, chosen by Detroit with their fourth pick in the 1989 draft, linked up with the Red Wings in Portland in July 1990, while the Soviet team was en route to Seattle for the Goodwill Games. He signaled his arrival in the NHL with a goal in New Jersey in his first game.

The language barrier fell almost as quickly. "At first I was kind of like a dog—I understand one or two words, like 'come here' or 'move'," remembers Fedorov. "Now I think in English and talk in English very naturally."

His first three seasons were a model of consistency—31 goals, 79 points, and a plus-11 mark

as a rookie, 32 goals, 86 points, plus-26 as a sophomore, 34, 87, and plus-33 in his third season. He was also instrumental in easing fellow Russians Vladimir Konstantinov and Slava Kozlov onto the team. "Fedorov was a valuable buffer for us when the other guys got here," says Detroit assistant coach Dave Lewis. "He broke the barrier. He'd picked up the language and could show these guys how it could be done."

It was his fourth year—the typical breakthrough season for an NHL player—in which Fedorov really blossomed on the ice, though. He chased Gretzky all year long for the Ross Trophy, finally finishing a close second with 120 points on 56 goals and 64 helpers. His plus-48 mark was also the NHL's second best. Fedorov was awarded the Hart Trophy as league MVP, the Selke as best defensive forward, NHL First All-Star Team honors, and, particularly meaningful to Fedorov, the Pearson Award for MVP as selected by his fellow players. He was the first Euro Soviet player to win any major NHL trophy other than the Calder.

Along with the hardware, the rave reviews just kept coming.

"Sergei is a game-breaker for us anytime he's on the ice," said teammate Steve Yzerman, now a 13-year veteran who himself ranks among the game's all-time greats. "He's the most talented player I've ever seen, and I don't think there's any reason why he shouldn't dominate every night."

In spite of 50 points in 42 games the next season (despite a separated shoulder), and in spite of league-leading assist and point totals in the 1995 playoffs, Fedorov's courage and intensity were questioned by some members of the media and his own team. The acquisition of Igor Larionov, center of the Soviets' fabulous KLM line of the 1980s, early in the 1995-96 season, was thought by some to be a ploy to improve Fedorov's play. "When I came to Army in 1986, I was just a kid," said Fedorov. "Igor was in his prime, was the best centerman to ever play hockey in the world. I watched him for four and a half years, how he played, how he practiced. I admired him through my hockey career. All of a sudden he ended up with Detroit after 10 years. You know how much excitement it would bring to any person who would grow up like that, watching their favourite players and work with them together on the same team, on the same ice?"

Larionov gave Detroit all the parts for the first all-Russian unit to play together in the NHL—Fedorov, Larionov, and Kozlov at forward,

Konstantinov and Soviet demigod Slava Fetisov on defence. Some old-guard factions thought it was too much; Red Wings right winger Doug Brown disagreed. "I feel that we're bringing in the best quality players. It doesn't matter what nationality or what anybody's ethnic background is."

"Forty-six Russian players were on NHL rosters to start this season," Fetisov pointed out. "The skill of the game is higher now. The image of the league is of players like Pavel Bure, Sergei Fedorov, and Alexander Mogilny. The way they play is exciting. The people recognize it, and it is what they come to see."

The arrival of Larionov moved Fedorov to the right wing; when the Red Wings found themselves short of defensemen midway through the year, Fedorov spent several games on the Detroit blue line. "He's such a talented skater, and his ability to skate backward so well helps him on defense," says Lewis. "People don't realize how tough a transition it is. There's a lot of responsibility, and very little room for error."

Despite the turmoil, Fedorov proved a better sniper than his critics, potting 39 goals and rolling up 107 points, and again excelling with a plus-49 mark, the NHL's second best after Konstantinov, who may well have been the league's best defenseman in '95-96. With a wealth of talent led by Fedorov, Detroit steamrolled to an NHL-record 62 wins.

"Every forward likes to score goals," says Fedorov. "There's no question about it. I suppose I would like to focus more on being a team. This sport is not like skiing, you know, where you are going by yourself. As far as I'm concerned, when the team wins, everybody has fun."

S ergei is a game-breaker for us anytime he's on the ice. He's the most talented player I've ever seen.

*TWO CLOSE FOR COMFORT-Detroit's Sergei Fedorov knocks the fire out of this Devil.*

# Alexander Mogilny

"IT'S EXCITING FOR FANS WHEN ALEX PLAYS WELL," SAYS VANCOUVER CANUCKS SUPERSTAR PAVEL BURE. HE inadvertently spoke volumes, for he was speaking of his equally stellar teammate, Alexander Mogilny, and no player is more readily acknowledged as one of hockey's most exciting, nor more frequently questioned as to how often he actually does play well.     What has never been questioned is Mogilny's emormous talent. A rare find from the far eastern reaches of the Soviet Union—Mogilny grew up in Khabarovsk, an industrial city of about half a million people on the Chinese border—he made his way to Moscow at 15, met the coach of the Central Army junior team at a practice session, wheedled a tryout from him, and impressed immediately. Mogilny stuck, and at 17 he was already a regular with the Army Elite League club.     Mogilny showcased his prodigious talent at the 1988 World Junior Championships in Moscow, exploding for nine goals and nine assists in only seven games. Although the Soviet juniors had to settle for the silver medal in their own backyard, the kid called "Sasha" was named the tournament's outstanding forward.     "He was such a talented guy—really good with the stick, and smart," recalls Igor Larionov, then the center on Army's magnificent KLM line and now a star with the Detroit Red Wings. "But he was kind of an unusual guy when he was a kid. You could see he was a big fan of western music, and I don't mean country. And he was the kind of guy who liked to dress up really well. The coach was making all the decisions, but he was a different guy—listening, then doing his own thing."     That modicum of independence was infuriating to Viktor Tikhonov, the tyrannical coach of CSKA and the Soviet national team for over 20 years. In the 1988 Calgary Olympics, the teenage Mogilny scored three times in six games as the Soviets wrapped up the gold medal early, but after taking a minor penalty in a meaningless tournament-closing loss to Finland he was actually slugged on the bench by Tikhonov.     Mogilny turned down an officer's commission, which would have bound him to Central Army, and found his request for a better apartment denied and himself left off a club tour of Japan. Later he accepted the nominal army position. Reinstated, he combined with linemates Bure and Sergei Fedorov to run amok at the 1989 World Juniors in Anchorage: all three members of the troika, anointed to succeed the aging KLM unit, racked up points in double figures as they cruised to gold.     In league play a month later, Mogilny pounded Spartak defenseman Yuri Yashin, who had high-sticked him earlier in the game. Mogilny was suspended, docked a month's pay, stripped of his Soviet Master of Sport honors.

*GOOOOOAAAAAALL!-The Ducks aren't quacking because Alexander Mogilny just scored.*

His perceived hot-dogging, trash-talking on-ice antics confounded the staid Soviet Ice Hockey Federation. "He loves himself more than the game. He is not committed," said SIHF general secretary Valentin Kozin. "It is my opinion that he will be out of hockey in two years."

He was out of Soviet hockey, anyway. The Buffalo Sabres had named Mogilny their fifth selection, 89th overall, in the previous year's Entry Draft, and at the close of the May 1989 World Championships in Stockholm, Mogilny made his break for the West. Sabres brass, aided by a shadowy character named Sergei Fomitjov, spirited Mogilny out of Sweden and into Buffalo. He became the first Soviet player to defect to North America.

Mogilny, wearing number 89, literally didn't waste a minute announcing his arrival in the NHL. Twenty seconds into the 1989-90 season opener, Mogilny pounced on a loose puck in the Quebec crease and tapped it home for his first goal. It was appropriate it came that quickly; Mogilny's phenomenal acceleration and flat-out speed soaring down the right wing would soon become his trademarks.

After counseling calmed his fear of flying, which caused him to miss several games at the end of his rookie year, Mogilny doubled his goal production to 30 in 1990-91. Pat LaFontaine's arrival in Buffalo the next season catapulted

Mogilny to 39 goals and All-Star status in '91-92.

There was no stopping the Sabres' dynamic duo in 1992-93. LaFontaine built a monster 148-point season with Mogilny alongside; Mogilny flashed down his wing, dug in the corners, absorbed a pounding in front of the net, and ripped terrified goaltenders for 50 goals in his first 46 games. He went on to total an astounding 76 goals on the year. "He was great to play with," says LaFontaine. "Those were two years I'll always remember."

Mogilny's goal-a-game pace carried into the playoffs, where the Sabres won their first series in a decade, but in Game 3 of the quarterfinals against Montreal, he was bowled over in a goalmouth scramble; his skate caught in a rut in the ice, twisting his right leg to a grotesque angle under him as he fell, snapping his shinbone and tearing ligaments in his ankle.

Upon Mogilny's return the next season, the Sabres tried to thrust responsibility upon him by giving him the captain's "C" in LaFontaine's injury-enforced absence, making him the first Russian-trained player ever to skipper an NHL team, but his performance was inconsistent. In November his fear of flying resurfaced. In March a confrontation with Fomitjov made headlines. Mogilny said his old acquaintance was trying to extort $150,000 with threats of violence; in court, Fomitjov said he was asking an old friend for a modest loan; he wound up deported. Mogilny dropped to 32 goals and 79 points, good marks but far below his standard.

The delayed 1994-95 season and the diplomatic efforts of Slava Fetisov gave Mogilny the

> I don't think scoring 76 goals again is out of the question. You never know, playing with Pavel I could score a hundred.

opportunity for a brief return to Russia and a reunion with family and friends early in 1995. He played one game for Spartak before returning to Buffalo, but managed just 19 goals in the shortened season and developed the damning reputation of a floater. In July he was traded to Vancouver for a raft of prospects.

For Mogilny, though, it was as if he'd escaped to freedom a second time. He relished the chance to play once more with Bure. "I am very excited about playing with Pavel," Mogilny said. "I don't think scoring 76 goals again is out of the question. You never know, playing with Pavel I could score a hundred."

The promise of the revived Russian connection helped boost season-ticket sales in Vancouver from 8,500 to 12,000, but soon Bure went down with a season-ending injury. Nevertheless, Mogilny carried on spectacularly, reestablishing himself as one of hockey's most feared marksmen.

Mogilny blasted 55 goals in 1995-96 and added a career-high 52 assists to go with a typically high plus-minus mark and low penalty total. It's anyone's guess how long he and the Canuck fans will stay happy together, but Mogilny claims his more mature attitude will make the situation work. "I learned a lot the last seven years—about people and myself and life in general. I've learned to protect myself from some things. The higher you go up, the harder you fall, so you keep your feet on the ground as much as possible."

As long as those feet keep moving at their supersonic speed, Mogilny will flourish as one of hockey's most exciting and one of its best.

# Alexei Yashin

HE COMES FROM SVERDLOVSK, 1,500 MILES EAST OF MOSCOW. HE'S A GIFTED ATHLETE WHO SEES A POST-hockey career in environmental engineering. He's a first-round draft choice who still took the NHL by surprise. He's a brilliant finesse player but with the size and strength of a power forward. He plays like a power forward yet rarely takes a penalty. He's a team-first guy who twice in three seasons has been embroiled in ugly contract hassles. He's resented by some as a puck hog, yet he's been named his team's most valuable player. ◉ That's Alexei Yashin, one of the most talented and exciting young players in hockey. A bundle of contradictions to many, Yashin seems undeterred by the detours and continues straight ahead on the road to stardom. ◉ Yashin was the expansion Ottawa Senators' first choice, the second player taken overall, in the 1992 Entry Draft. A member of the Soviet gold-medal-winning team in the 1992 World Junior Championships, he turned in an impressive campaign for Dinamo Moscow in 1992-93. He was a force for Russia in their World Championship triumph in Munich in 1993. Yet, despite all of this, Yashin didn't receive the hype that was cranked up for other young stars with similarly glowing resumes. He was still an unknown quantity to most of the NHL at the start of the 1993-94 season. ◉ It didn't take long before Yashin showed them what he could do. Still only 19, he needed just 11 games before scoring his first NHL hat trick, adding two assists as he led Ottawa to a win in Edmonton. Two nights later, on his 20th birthday, he set up four more goals, leading the Senators to victory in Winnipeg. Suddenly, everyone was watching, and he hasn't been out of the spotlight since. ◉ A superb stickhandler with a repertoire of baffling moves, the one knock on Yashin's game may be his skating. But he showed veteran savvy by using his 6-3, 216-pound size to head into traffic instead of away from it, slowing down the play to control it at his own pace, then bulling his way to the net, stickhandling back out of the scrum himself, or setting up teammates with a seeing-eye pass. "He's not the skater most Europeans are," observed Rick Bowness, then Ottawa's coach, "and the smaller ice surface helps him. Plus he's big and strong and protects the puck well." ◉ Like many European players, whose schedules are usually less than half the length of the NHL season, Yashin worried about the rigors of the interminable NHL schedule, although he had actually played 110 games the previous season with Dinamo and the Russian national team. "My work is different," he said. "It's not easy to play in Canada, not easy to play all the time. NHL is very difficult." ◉ But he adjusted immediately to NHL play, and it came as no surprise to his coaches. "Our scouts said he'd probably be a better North American player than he was a European," noted Senators assistant coach E.J. McGuire.

Yashin continued to play so well, in fact, that he was Ottawa's lone representative in the NHL All-Star Game, the only rookie to participate in the contest. He more than rose to the occasion by scoring two goals, including the dramatic winner with less than four minutes to play, in the Eastern Conference's come-from-behind victory.

"I don't think I can remember a young guy joining the league and making the impact he's making," said former Hartford coach Pierre McGuire. "I'm not sure the people really know just how good he is. A guy like Yashin can carry a team."

Confirming McGuire's suspicion, Yashin was not the first choice in the voting for the Calder Trophy, in spite of finishing the season with team-leading numbers—30 goals and 49 assists in 83 games, just three points behind Mikael Renberg for the NHL rookie scoring title, with only 22 penalty minutes. Ottawa had repeated as the league's worst team; he was one of only three Senators to manage more than 26 points on the year. Yashin was unconcerned with individual honors, saying his season "was okay. I'd be more happy if the Senators played better and had a higher place in the standings. I try to do everything I can for the Senators."

Nevertheless, the team's young MVP found himself engaged in a contract squabble with the Ottawa front office after the season and through the labor dispute that delayed the start of the '94-95 campaign. Yashin dabbled briefly with the Las Vegas team in the International League

I'm not sure the people really know just how good he is. A guy like Yashin can carry a team.

and spent time with his close-knit family. Both of Yashin's parents were elite athletes in the Soviet Union in the 1960s and '70s; his mother, a former volleyball player, is an electrical engineer, and his father, a former team handball player, is a professor of environmental engineering. It's no wonder, then, that Yashin is an excellent student as well as a star athlete, and looks toward engineering when his hockey career is over.

The season finally began, but without Yashin in Ottawa's training camp; the team's only contract concessions were a promise to renegotiate if certain team goals were met. Yashin returned. "I just try to do my work really well," he claimed. "I try to help my friends on the team. I like to play on this team, I don't want a trade to another team. All we need is hard work and to correct our mistakes."

Yashin rifled in 17 goals in the first half of the shortened season, nearly a third of the entire team's output. He wound up with nearly a point a game, leading the Senators in every major offensive category.

"A lot of people don't know how good this kid is," Bowness stated. "He's a great competitor and a solid, solid team guy. They say there are players who are worth the price of admission. Well, he's one of them." But Ottawa was again the NHL's weakest team, and the Senators again refused to revise Yashin's contract.

That finally prompted Yashin to go AWOL as the 1995-96 season began; he even returned briefly to Russia to play a couple of games for the great Central Army team in Moscow, while rookie Daniel Alfredsson took a turn at trying to carry the entire Senator attack. Yashin finally rejoined

Ottawa around the midway point of the season, and despite the rust of a nine-month absence, again produced almost a point a game, finishing second on the club in scoring while playing barely half the schedule. Although the team finished as the NHL's worst for the fourth time in its four-year existence, their performance in the second half of the season showed marked improvement, thanks to the mid year installation of a new general manager and coach and the addition of Yashin, giving Ottawa fans hope for imminent relief from the torture. Yashin remains the man they'll count on to lift them from their Slough of Despond.

"He's a franchise player," says former Senators goalie Craig Billington. "He's right up there now in the top echelon of players. And you know what? He's only going to get better."

*LIVING SINGLE-All alone on the Garden ice, Ottawa's Alexei Yashin begins the Senators' rush.*

# Sergei Zubov

FOR ALL THE GREAT FORWARDS THE FORMER SOVIET UNION HAS PRODUCED OVER THE YEARS, IT HAS SPAWNED precious few great defensemen. The best Soviet teams of the '70s and '80s, with their relentless, swirling rushes, their laser-beam passes, the 0-to-60 acceleration of their skating, were spectacular—but on those rare occasions when they lost, their Achilles heel was always defense. Who can forget that they blew a 3-games-to-1 lead in the fabled 1972 Summit Series, and a two-goal lead in the third period of the deciding match—including Paul Henderson's series-winning tally in the very last minute off a giveaway in their own end? Or that the 1980 U.S. Olympic team's Miracle on Ice was enabled by sloppy defensive work around the Soviet crease? Or that Mario Lemieux's Canada Cup–winning goal in 1987 was made possible when a defenseman simply fell down, allowing a Canadian three-on-one break in the final 90 seconds? 🏒 The game as it was played in the old Soviet Union, and as it continues to be played on the spacious ice surfaces of its successor states today, emphasizes attack, not defense. Thus you can count the great blueliners the old USSR produced on, well, two fingers: Viacheslav Fetisov, who starred for CSKA and the Soviet national team from 1974 through 1989, defied the authorities by jumping to New Jersey, and shone on with Detroit as late as 1996; and Alexei Kasatonov, his longtime defense partner with CSKA and the Devils. Today, only a handful of those who came of age in the twilight of the Soviet era show signs of blossoming into true defense stars, like Russia's Vladimir Konstantinov, Latvia's Sandis Ozolinsh, or Ukraine's Alexei Zhitnik. 🏒 But one Soviet-trained defender, at the still tender age of 26, has already proven himself as one of the very best his country has ever produced. His name: Sergei Zubov. 🏒 A swift skater with dazzling passing skills and an abundance of ideas in the attacking zone, Zubov scores a lot, prevents his foes from scoring, and does so while taking very few penalties—a dream package of talents virtually impossible to find in one player. Zubov is, simply, one of the best defensemen to debut on this continent in this decade. And yet he has always played in someone else's shadow. In New York, where he started his NHL career in 1992-93, it was the brilliant rearguard Brian Leetch who always got the headlines. After being traded to Pittsburgh in August 1995, Zubov was overshadowed by the incomparable Mario Lemieux, not to mention scoring aces Jaromir Jagr and Ron Francis. With his 1996 trade to Dallas, maybe now there will be more of a spotlight for him. 🏒 His ability deserves more recognition. Zubov played three years with the Rangers, including a '93-94 campaign in which he led the team in

*3, 2, 1, CONTACT-
Pittsburgh's Sergei Zubov
prepares to unleash his
deadly slap shot.*

scoring. He thus became the first defenseman in NHL history ever to pace a regular-season champion. "It was surprising to me to play like that," he said. "Then I just got used to it. I mean, I have to get points when I play with guys like Leetch and Messier." That June, Zubov—along with teammates Aleksander Karpovtsev, Sergei Nemchinov, and Alexei Kovalev—also became one of the first four Russians ever to have his name inscribed on the Stanley Cup.

Even in his career in Russia, where he began with CSKA at age 18, Zubov didn't attract the attention his teammates Pavel Bure, Sergei Fedorov,

and Valeri Kamensky drew. But he learned how to generate offense from the blue line from Fetisov, his boyhood idol, with whom he spent a half year at CSKA. Zubov went on to help the Army team to their 13th straight Elite League title in '89, the national junior team to a World Championship that same year, and the Olympic team to a gold medal in '92 (during those Olympics he was not on the ice for a single even-strength goal-against). On either continent, in domestic play or international, Zubov has always excelled.

As a very young boy in Moscow, he learned the game with Karpovtsev. "We were in school together," remembers Zubov. "His home was maybe 500 meters from my house. The first year in school he said, 'Let's go. I know a place we can really play hockey.'" By age seven the future Ranger defensemen were youth league teammates, and would continue to play together for years.

Zubov also often played against another childhood friend, Pavel Bure. Many years later they would face each other again, but for much higher stakes—the Stanley Cup. Zubov and Bure had several thrilling one-on-one duels during the '94 Cup Final. Both were brilliant in that memorable series, but Zubov had some especially transcendent moments. His slap shot in the final seconds of the second period tied Game 4, which the Rangers went on to win. And in Game 7 his millimeter-precise pass to Brian Leetch helped give the Rangers a 1–0 lead, which soon became 2–0 when Zubov rushed past two Canucks to set up a scoring play.

In the jubilant dressing room after the game, there seemed to be almost as many Russian-speaking revelers as English-speakers. Homesickness is often a problem for players who come to North America from Europe, but it wasn't for Zubov. Like the other Russian Rangers, he felt very much at home among New York's large population of Russian emigres. North America's biggest concentration of recent arrivals from the former USSR can be found in the Brighton Beach section of Brooklyn, about a 45 minute subway ride from Madison Square Garden. Zubov's family and friends spent many evenings in "Little Odessa," as Brighton Beach is often called—including one unforgettable June 1994 night

I never felt something like that even at the Olympics. When you win the Stanley Cup, you're the best in the world.

after the Rangers captured the Stanley Cup. Zubov, Kovalev, Nemchinov, and Karpovtsev rented out a famed Russian banquet hall for a borscht-, caviar-, and vodka-drenched victory party that roared on till all hours.

Despite being bothered by an old wrist injury that forced him to miss 10 games, Zubov played well for the Rangers in the abbreviated '95 season, winding up third in points-per-game among the league's defensemen. Alongside Leetch, he continued to co-anchor a Ranger power play widely regarded as the league's best. Their crisp passing on the points was a wonder to behold, and their shooting was deadly accurate. "I compare Sergei to a Denis Potvin," said then-teammate Kevin Lowe, "the way he controls the game at his speed, the way he passes the puck, the way he shoots, and the way he stands in there and makes the big plays offensively."

The Zubov-Leetch partnership finally came to an end before the '95-96 season, when the Penguins dealt to get him from the Rangers. Zubov carved out an important niche on that explosive roster. He was the Pens' top-scoring defenseman, and his 1.05 points-per-game ratio was number two among NHL rearguards, an eyelash behind—who else?—Brian Leetch. But the playoffs ended in disappointment with Pittsburgh's defeat in the semifinals. Amid reports of friction between Lemieux and Zubov, the Russian was dealt again, this time to Dallas. Perhaps there he will be able to relive the thrill of 1994: "I never felt something like that even at the Olympics," says Zubov. "When you win the Stanley Cup, you understand that you're the best in the world."

# Sweden and Finland

In 1972, the Russians opened North American eyes to just how entertaining and effective the finesse-oriented European style of hockey could be. The Soviet team's shocking success against the very best from Canada served notice that a sea-change was imminent in the way hockey was played on this side of the Atlantic. But it was the Scandinavians who made the first forays onto North American rinks as members of major league professional teams. And it was they who showed the North Americans, on a nightly basis, how it was done.

The first Scandinavians to perform regularly in the NHL (Finnish forward Juha Widing in 1969, Swedish defenseman Thommie Bergman in '72) distinguished themselves as good players, but did not freewheel in the European style. But the next notable import, defenseman Borje Salming, did. Signed by Toronto along with fellow Swede Inge Hammarstrom, Salming was an elegant puck carrier with a hard, accurate shot who was also very steady in his own end. But Salming and Hammarstrom's presence on the Leafs brought to the fore a bizarre ethnic antagonism. Their reluctance to fight and their preference for simply recapturing the puck without driving their man through the boards earned them the label "chicken Swedes." No matter that Salming played through several serious, even grotesque injuries and would enjoy an esteemed 17-year NHL career—the aspersion against all Scandinavian players still persists today in certain quarters.

But it was the WHA that provided the fertile ground in which the Eurostyle would flower. In 1974 the Winnipeg Jets signed Swedish forwards Anders Hedberg and Ulf Nilsson to play alongside legendary superstar Bobby Hull. The three clicked immediately, each tallying over 100 points, with Hull scoring 77 goals in 78 games, and romped through the rebel league for the following three years. As a team, the Jets were pioneers in the European style: their '75-76 roster included the then unheard-of total of nine players from Sweden and Finland; they trained in those two countries and in Czechoslovakia, and even traveled to Moscow for the Izvestia Cup. The Jets were rewarded by winning three WHA championships in the league's remaining four years.

In '78, Hedberg and Nilsson signed with the Rangers, propelling them to the Stanley Cup Final and signaling the NHL's full embrace of the European style. Scoring rose dramatically leaguewide as defenses struggled to cope with the dazzling kaleidoscope of centers and wingers that swirled around them. Scandinavians were key performers throughout the '80s and into the '90s: flashy scorers like Kent Nilsson; great two-way forwards like Mats Naslund, Hakan Loob, and Thomas Steen; playmaking defensemen like Reijo Ruotsalainen; Stanley Cup–fixture blueliners like the Islanders' Stefan Persson and Tomas Jonsson; stellar goalies like Pelle Lindbergh; agitating win-at-all-cost types like Tomas Sandstrom or, with his three Cup rings with the Oilers and one with the Rangers, Esa Tikkanen. But the greatest of them all was Finnish right winger Jari Kurri, who formed a fruitful scoring partnership with linemate Wayne Gretzky for most of his illustrious career. The NHL's seventh leading all-time goal-scorer, Kurri's centrality to the Oilers' five Stanley Cup–winning teams is not merely summed up by his status as the league's No. 3 all-time playoff goal scorer and No. 3 in all-time postseason points. He has also earned a reputation as a great checker—further evidence that Scandinavians excel at every phase of the game.

Finland has also made its mark on the league in the record-shattering form of Teemu Selanne, who became the first rookie ever voted to the NHL's First All-Star Team at right wing. When Selanne joined the Mighty Ducks, he helped turn the worst power play in the league into a fearsome engine of destruction. The Finnish Flash has thrived in both hemispheres as a hockey star and local hero, idolized from Helsinki to Winnipeg to Anaheim.

Today, one of every six players in the NHL is Russian or European, ample demonstration of how profound has been the impact of the Euro-Soviet style on these shores. Yet despite the exodus of so much young talent to the U.S. and Canada, national programs remain strong: Finland won silver at the 1988 Olympics and Sweden took Olympic gold in Lillehammer in 1994. Scandinavia continues to produce many of the world's greatest players, and it is the good fortune of North Americans to be able to watch them nightly on the rinks of the NHL.

# Daniel Alfredsson

EVERY FEW YEARS, A TEENAGE PHENOM GOES ON A SCORING RAMPAGE IN JUNIOR HOCKEY AND IS HYPED as a can't-miss prospect, the next NHL superstar. Perreault, Dionne, Lafleur, Gretzky, LaFontaine, Lemieux, Lindros, Forsberg—they all lived up to that billing. Almost as often, though, these highly touted junior stars only achieve mediocre status in the pros; some never make a mark in the NHL at all. *But* every few years, too, some completely unheralded player skates onto the NHL scene and turns out to be just the sort of star every team hopes to draft. *In the 1995–96 season, Daniel Alfredsson of the Ottawa Senators, with only a handful of career highlights on his audition videotape, chosen 133rd overall in the 1994 Entry Draft, was that sort of player. *Even in his native Sweden, Alfredsson wasn't counted on to be an Elite League player. He'd been a defenseman until he was almost 15, when he was put on the right wing. He remained a solid but unexceptional performer until he blossomed in 1993–94 with an MVP season for Vasta Frolunda. Husky, but without the "power forward" size so much in vogue in the NHL; quick, but without straightaway speed; Alfredsson drew little attention from North American scouts even when his overtime goal in the 1995 World Championships knocked Canada out of the tournament and helped Sweden to the silver medal. *Unsure whether his game was of sufficient caliber for the NHL, Alfredsson consulted his Swedish teammates. "I talked to some of the guys who had played here and I felt this year I was old enough," says Alfredsson. "I had no NHL expectations. I'd never even played in a world junior. I had no thoughts of being drafted." *When Alfredsson joined last-place Ottawa for 1995–96, even the Senators themselves didn't expect him to make the team. But he did, and he made an impact. Without help from the team's two young star centermen—Alexei Yashin was embroiled in a contract hassle and Alexandre Daigle was mired in a slump—Alfredsson and some strong goaltending led the team to a surprising 6–5–0 start, including wins against powerhouses like the Rangers and Red Wings. Alfredsson served notice he came to play in Game 12 with his first NHL hat trick. *Rick Bowness, who began the year as the Senators' coach, said, "From the first day here, he competed. He takes hits and he gives hits. He has the desire to compete. It's a lot more than just skill." *Inevitably, the lack of depth and skill on the rest of the team wasted their promising start, and Alfredsson's continued excellence turned out to be

the one bright spot for Ottawa fans. The Senators fired their general manager and two coaches as another last-place campaign ground on.

Alfredsson rose above the turmoil. "I had five coaches when I played in Sweden," he said. "It's been tough, you don't want to have too many changes, but sometimes things have to happen."

What happened was a very fine year for Alfredsson individually: he led a tight race for NHL rookie scoring, and won the Calder Trophy; he was Ottawa's lone representative in the NHL All-Star Game; and he earned accolades from both the parade of coaches who walked behind the Ottawa bench and players and coaches around the league.

Dave Allison, who took over from Bowness, said of Alfredsson, "He plays 24 to 30 minutes a game in all situations, and that's a testament to how good he is. It says he came over here and has worked hard to play at a high level. That's due to his professionalism and his attention to the day-to-day details."

"He's a character kid," says Florida Panthers general manager Bryan Murray. "He's not the best skater in the world, but he gives every ounce of what he's got."

"He's the only guy who can go through five guys on the other team," says Chico Resch, the former Islander goalie, now an assistant coach in Ottawa. The Senators' strategy, he says, became "get the puck to Alfie. He's the

> He takes hits and he gives hits. He has the desire to compete. It's a lot more than just skill.

complete package. Good defensively, great hockey sense offensively. If he were playing with a slick center, he'd score 40 goals."

"He's got a temper," adds Resch. "When he gets mad, he hits you but it's not like he runs all over the ice to smash somebody. He's a Canadian-style player. He got hit in the face with a puck in Vancouver and kept playing."

Alfredsson's willingness to go into the corners and his constant-motion style, his ability to anticipate the play and to slip past checks, have drawn comparisons to fellow Swedes Hakan Loob and Thomas Steen, who starred in the NHL through the 1980s.

"I like to be a player at both ends and work hard," says Alfredsson. "I want to play defense and then, like everybody else, capitalize on the chances when you get them."

"It's fun to score goals," he states. "That's what the game is all about."

But, he adds, "I try not to think about the points that I make. The most important thing is what I can contribute to the team. We have a young, talented team. We are learning every game. We have to keep progressing as players and as a team, and then things will turn around."

Current Senators coach Jacques Martin knows Alfredsson's presence will help at last to make that a possibility in Ottawa. "He's a tremendous player and has so many dimensions. He's responsible and works hard—and he's team-oriented. He's a great kid to build around."

*THE SINGLE GUY-Ottawa's Daniel Alfredsson is all alone as he waits for the puck.*

# Peter Forsberg

WHEN HE WAS ONLY 16, HOCKEY COGNOSCENTI SAID PETER FORSBERG WOULD BE AN NHL SUPERSTAR—AND they were right. It took less than two seasons of NHL action for Forsberg to be so anointed. Now, he and underrated superstar Joe Sakic give the Colorado Avalanche the most potent one-two punch this side of Mario Lemieux and Jaromir Jagr. ⬤ It all started in Forsberg's final season of Swedish junior play with MoDo, when he notched 38 goals and 102 points in just 39 games. Philadelphia made him the sixth pick overall in the 1991 Entry Draft. Only one amateur player generated a more raucous clamor among scouts and coaches at that draft: Eric Lindros. One year later, the Flyers dealt Forsberg, two established stars in goaltender Ron Hextall and defenseman Steve Duchesne, three additional players, two future first-round draft picks, cash, Ventnor Avenue and both Utilities, the kitchen sink, and a partridge in a pear tree, all to the Quebec Nordiques for the rights to Lindros. ⬤ The anticipation surrounding Forsberg was momentarily eclipsed by the Lindros hype, but once the Flyer colossus was bestriding NHL arenas, observers of future prospects returned their gaze to Sweden. Forsberg turned it on for the scouts with an eye-popping performance in the 1993 World Junior Championships, earning the award as the tournament's outstanding forward. ⬤ He had moved up to the MoDo Elite League team, and he saved his best for the 1994 playoffs, cranking out nine goals and 16 points in 11 games, leading his eighth-place club to the playoff final. "Forsberg was the reason MoDo did so well," said Toronto scout and former Ranger star Anders Hedberg. "He was clearly the leader of that team." ⬤ Those performances were enough to make young Forsberg a Swedish hockey legend, but it was his heroics in the 1994 Winter Olympics in Lillehammer, Norway, that earned him a place amongst the Norse gods. Forsberg started slowly but became more of a force as the Olympics went along, at last leading Sweden to the Gold Medal game against Canada. The championship game wound up tied and it was left to the bizarre spectacle of a penalty-shot contest to decide the outcome. It was Forsberg who snapped home the melodramatic winning goal, earning Sweden its first-ever Olympic Gold Medal in hockey. ⬤ Amid all the other attendant accolades in recognition of the feat, Forsberg became the first hockey player ever to appear on a Swedish postage stamp. It may have been the last chance for opponents to find some way to lick the kid. ⬤ The Swedish fans and sporting press gnashed their teeth and tore their hair when Forsberg left after the Elite League playoffs, passing up a standing invitation to represent Sweden in the World Championships and instead reporting

*SLIP SLIDING AWAY-*
*Colorado's Peter Forsberg is*
*slipping but the puck is still*
*sliding.*

to the Nordiques.

"I have to laugh at all the commotion." Forsberg said. "I have no reason to feel guilty. I gave it my best shot at the Olympics and I think I did everything for my country then. Hockey in Sweden is now a thing of the past for me. I wanted to see first hand how hockey is played over here. As soon as my season ended with my MoDo team. I became a full-time member of the Quebec

Nordiques. a North American professional."

A cellar-dwelling franchise for years. Les Nordiques had garnered high draft picks that they used wisely to accumulate a stable of prime young talent ready to make an impact in the NHL and launch the team out of the basement. The addition of Forsberg provided the critical mass necessary for that explosion—an expectation that placed extra weight on so highly touted a first-round selection. one already having to deal with a different style of hockey in a new country.

Forsberg seemed oblivious to the pressure. A slick skater with great balance and tremendous acceleration. he read the ice well. charged into traffic. and became a regular on the penalty-killing unit. Forsberg's approach and attitude were never in question. but his offensive production early in the season was as wan as the Swedish winter sun. and he had yet to show the chippy. physical presence that had been one of his trademarks in Scandinavia.

"It's a big jump for me." Forsberg conceded. "I played more physical back home—more dirty. I played on a lousy team and we were always behind in games. I would get crazy and run at guys. On this team we have four good lines and we're usually ahead by a couple of goals. I don't get as angry."

He had little reason to be angry. After three or four weeks in the NHL. Forsberg had learned what most players need three or four years to absorb.

"After about Game 10. he really found the league." said Nordiques coach Marc Crawford. "There's a huge adjustment from playing in Europe. In North America there's much tighter checking. it's more physical. there's a lot of forechecking pressure so you are pressured with the puck. Once he figured that out. he came up with ways to combat that. He not only was one of the best rookies in the league. by the end of the year he was one of the best players in the league."

That's one way to describe Forsberg's performance down the stretch—12 goals and 24 assists over the season's last 27 games. He finished with

a plus-17 mark, and his final total of 50 points in 47 games gave him the rookie scoring title and earned him the Calder Trophy.

"I certainly don't see myself as a franchise player." said Forsberg. whose excruciating modesty stands in odd contrast to his brash on-ice confidence. Did he see a league scoring title in his future? "No. never. That is for the great players."

After his sophomore year. in which the Nords relocated to Denver and became the Colorado Avalanche. even Forsberg may have to change his thinking on that one. He trailed only the Penguins' dynamic duo of Lemieux and Jagr atop the list of NHL scoring leaders for most of the 1995–96 campaign.

"Success won't change him. but he's going to have to come to grips with the fact he is a star." says Crawford. "He's almost too humble. but on the ice he competes as well as anybody. I think you're going to see Peter come more and more out of his shell when he becomes more comfortable with the language and his [fame]."

Forsberg's superior balance and wide skating stance make it almost impossible to knock him off his feet. and enable him to protect the puck while he looks to dish off his next smart. accurate pass. Yet the 5-11. 190-pound Forsberg can muck and grind along the boards as well. and thrives on the physical game.

"You see some skill players who don't normally get involved physically." says Colorado general manager Pierre Lacroix. "Not Peter. He hits so hard it is unbelievable."

"He's strong. he battles every step of the way. and he has very gifted offensive skills." Crawford sums up. "Peter is just doing it all."

# Nicklas Lidstrom

NICKLAS LIDSTROM WILL TALK ABOUT HOCKEY. HE'LL TELL YOU ABOUT DETROIT'S LAST GAME OR THEIR next and analyze the opposition. He'll tell you how great his teammates are and who's helped his career. He'll tell you about his wife and young son. But he won't tell you how good he is. You'll have to listen to everyone else say it for him.  Quiet, pleasant, intelligent, modest, the epitome of the Swedish hockey player, Lidstrom goes all but unnoticed as one of the most skilled and effective blueliners in hockey. "Nicklas comes to the rink, puts in a good night at the office, and goes home," says Red Wings assistant general manager Ken Holland. "You hardly even know he's in the room sometimes."  "When I first started out," remembers Lidstrom, a native of Vasteras, Sweden, "I just wanted to play on the big team in my home town. When I was 13 or 14, I wanted to play in the Elite League. It wasn't until I was about 16 that I started to think about the NHL. That's pretty much when everybody started talking about it. Then when I got drafted, I knew I had a chance to play in the NHL."  The Detroit Red Wings chose Lidstrom with their third pick in the 1989 Entry Draft. He spent two more seasons with Vasteras in the Swedish Elite League, but knew he had more than just a chance in the NHL after playing for his country in the 1991 World Championships, where Sweden won the gold medal, and in the 1991 Canada Cup. "We played head-to-head against Canada, the U.S.," says Lidstrom. "I realized then that I could play in the NHL. I thought that in that tournament the game would be so much better in every aspect. But I could skate with them."  Although top-flight defensemen usually need years of experience to develop, and despite the twin handicaps of the smaller North American rinks and a slight language barrier, Lidstrom was a highly effective performer for Detroit from the very start.  "It's a little tough on the ice at first," says Lidstrom, who bears a slight resemblance to actor Christian Slater. "You aren't used to yelling in English on the ice, so at first you are just reacting. You are thinking in Swedish and slowly translating into English.  "I had to simplify my game. I had to play safe, minimize mistakes, and get rid of the puck a lot quicker. That's why I always try to be in the right position, because I'm not going to go out and put the big hit on someone. That's just not my game.  "People are always looking for the big hits," says the 6-2, 180-pound Lidstrom, "but that's not what I'm all about. I'm not the biggest guy out there, so most of the time if I did try to crush somebody I would probably lose. I still take my guy out, but I do it in a different way."  Lidstrom

*THE POSTMAN-Detroit's Nicklas Lidstrom prepares to deliver the puck to an open teammate.*

learned much of his sterling defensive play as a rookie paired with veteran Brad McCrimmon, one of the premier defensive rearguards of the last generation. "He's more the stay-at-home kind of defenseman," says Lidstrom, "but I think we still complemented each other." There

was really no question: McCrimmon, at plus-39, and Lidstrom, at plus-36, had the second- and third-best plus-minus marks in the NHL that year. Lidstrom added 60 points' worth of offense as well, and finished as runner-up to Pavel Bure for the Calder Trophy.

Since then, Lidstrom's career has been a paradigm of reliability and consistency. He played his first 284 NHL games without a miss until a back injury late in the 1995 season cost him just five games. He chipped in 56 points in 1993-94 and his plus-43 mark was again among the NHL's top three. As Lidstrom says, "One thing I learned when I first came over here—as a defenseman you have to be consistent all the time, don't have too many ups and downs."

The ups have been steady, the downs almost nonexistent. "He has just got better and better," says Detroit coach Scotty Bowman. "He has great lateral movement, he can skate, and he has really good offensive sense. . . . He's one of the most underrated defensemen in the league."

Lidstrom, smooth and fast on his skates and superbly accurate with his shot and his passes, can play either side on defense, and on the power play is an asset at the point with his soccer-born ability to keep the puck in the attacking zone with his feet. "He's great at the blueline," says Detroit scout Hakan Andersson. "I've never seen a defenseman move sideways as quickly as Nick can. He can take a pass at one end of the blueline and be 12 to 15 feet over within one second."

For the last couple of years, Lidstrom has mostly been paired with Paul Coffey, one of the great puck-rushing, scoring defensemen in NHL history. Coffey likes the situation, saying, "We both move the puck, we're both good with the puck, and we're good with each other. We think the same way. The last weapon in our playbook is to bank the puck off the boards."

I'm not going to go out and put the big hit on someone. That's just not my game.

"When we play, we always talk a lot in between shifts," Lidstrom says of their partnership. "We'll talk about the way a particular pass went off and just about everything that happened during our shift. We communicate with each other very well and I think that is what makes us so good together. We're both skating a lot, trying to move all the time. I just try to hit him with the puck when he's moving."

The only thing the Red Wings want to see more of from Lidstrom is a leadership presence, another challenge Lidstrom quietly accepts. "It's a good feeling," he says. "They want me to step up more, and I think I have to do that. I've never been a big talker in the room. I have to show it on the ice instead."

Former teammate Mike Ramsey, another great veteran defensive blueliner, says of Lidstrom, "It's refreshing to see an athlete who's just down-to-earth, somebody that doesn't think the world owes him something. Some people like to be in the limelight, they want to be on TV every day. Other people are happy sitting in the shadow, being their own man. I'm sure he'd love to get the recognition that he deserves. But you're not going to see him go out and pound the drums for it."

"That's the one thing that might keep Nick from superstardom," says Andersson. "He's such a laid-back kind of guy. If he had the same kind of drive, the same mentality as Chris Chelios or Ray Bourque . . . If he had that drive, that he wanted to be a No. 1 star, who knows how good he'd be?"

It doesn't seem he or any defenseman could be much better than Lidstrom already is.

# Ulf Samuelsson

SWEDISH PLAYERS AREN'T TOUGH. THEY'RE FINE AT PLAYING FINESSE HOCKEY, BUT WHEN THE GOING gets rugged, they disappear. So goes the conventional wisdom in North America, and it's what many Canadians and Americans also think of Finns, Russians, Czechs, Slovaks, and any other European player. Ulf Samuelsson exposes the fallacy in that gross generalization. He's big and mean and rugged, and in a dozen years in the NHL he's proven to be perhaps the most punishingly effective stay-at-home defenseman of the current era. Whether playing with small-market Hartford early in his career, flashy Pittsburgh in the middle, or the glamorous Rangers as he embarks on the latter stages, Samuelsson has always been a tower of ornery strength on the blue line. He makes bitter enemies of opponents wherever he goes—and loyal friends of teammates appreciative of his commitment to victory. "I'll do anything to win," he says . . . and he means it. Samuelsson grew up in the steel town of Fagersta, Sweden, idolizing Toronto defenseman Borje Salming, one of the first Europeans to play regularly in the NHL, and one of the most successful ever. Salming was a high-scoring defender who rarely made a mistake in his own end in his 16 years with the Maple Leafs, an exemplary player tough enough to take a horrifying 300-stitch gash that zigzagged from foreheard to mouth and blithely quip: "Oh well, there goes my pretty face." But he did not rely on heavy bodychecking to shut down opposing forwards, and was accused of being one of the Swedes who, in gruff Leaf owner Harold Ballard's words, "could go into the corner with six eggs in his pocket and not break any of them." But though Samuelsson admired the skillful Salming, he did not emulate his style of play. Instead, young Ulf spent his boyhood years skating around his hometown rink hacking, whacking, and pounding—and getting hacked, whacked, and pounded by—his friend Tomas Sandstrom, another rambunctious Swede who has had a long, prosperous, and controversial NHL career. The two boys starred for their town team playing rugged, physical hockey, often appalling fans used to the more swirling, wide-open style of the European game. Hartford scouts, on the other hand, loved the way Samuelsson played, and drafted him in the fourth round of the 1982 Entry Draft. Arriving in North America as an eager 20-year-old in 1984, he made an immediate impression as an AHL rookie. After cutting an opponent with a high-stick, the victim's teammates took vengeance in their next game by jumping Samuelsson during warmups. Seven policemen and a police dog were needed to break up the melee. Halfway through the season he was called up to Hartford for good. He quickly won a

*FRIENDS- The Rangers' Ulf Samuelsson tries to control the rolling puck while his teammates look on.*

reputation as a hard-hitting defenseman. Unlike Salming and so many other Europeans playing in the NHL, whose courage was measured in accepting physical punishment to set up odd-man rushes, power plays, and goals, Samuelsson doled out punishment in a more traditionally North American way: he'd lay the lumber on you, cream you in open ice, and staple you to the boards—and forget the consequences.

Some foes thought Samuelsson hit too hard, or, to put it more accurately, too illegally. There was

an unfortunate incident involving Montreal's nifty Pierre Mondou in which Mondou suffered a career-ending cut on the eye when Samuelsson's stick nicked him—accidentally, according to the rookie Swede. Throughout the late '80s, Samuelsson had a running feud with Cam Neely, Boston's star winger, that came to a head in the '91 semifinals. Samuelsson, just acquired by the Penguins to shore up their defense for a Stanley Cup run, submarined Neely in open ice, and later jammed his knee into Neely's thigh during a collision along the boards. Samuelsson maintained both were legal checks, Neely and the Bruins felt otherwise; either way, Neely wound up suffering a leg injury that kept him out of action for virtually two years. Other famous encounters involving Samuelsson followed on through the '90s, usually with the 6-1, 200-pound Swede leaving foes sprawled and woozy on the ice—but not always. In October '95, in Samuelsson's fifth game as a Ranger, Toronto enforcer Tie Domi knocked Samuelsson unconscious with a bare-fisted blind-side punch. In the hours before the league slapped an eight-game suspension on Domi, Islanders defenseman Mathieu Schneider was asked how the Leaf should be dealt with for having leveled Samuelsson. "For hitting Ulf?" responded Schneider. "A bonus."

Samuelsson may be despised by many of those who've played against him, but he's always taken it with a ready wit. "Whenever I close my eyes," Samuelsson deadpanned while recovering from a 1987 concussion suffered in a collision with Quebec's Robert Picard, "I see little Picards running around everywhere." When feisty boyhood pal Sandstrom was about to join the Penguins in '94, Samuelsson warned: "You think I'm bad, wait till you get a load of Tomas." And just after the '95 season, when a *Sports Illustrated* poll asked him to name the NHL's dirtiest player, Samuelsson replied: "Can you vote for yourself?" By the way, Samuelsson won the poll hands down.

But all the controversy tends to obscure just how stalwart a defenseman Samuelsson really is. He led the Whalers in plus/minus a remarkable four years in a row, then ranked among the top three

We've got more guys going over to the tough play because they see that he's doing so well here.

in that category in all four of his seasons in Pittsburgh—an incredible feat, considering he's never scored more than nine goals or 33 assists in a single season. What it means in real terms is that practically no one from the other team ever scores while Samuelsson is on the ice. When the Penguins acquired him on March 4, 1991, observers predicted that his rock-steady defense would finally allow Mario Lemieux and company the freedom to wheel up ice without worrying about the consequences. They were right: the Pens, with the new-found security in their own end that Samuelsson provided, went on to capture the franchise's first-ever Stanley Cup, then repeated the feat a year later. So coveted is he for his defensive skills that he has to be the only hockey player with a mere 45 goals in his first 800 games to earn a $2 million-per-year contract.

No longer as high-strung as when he was a young player—one night when he was ejected from a Hartford-Toronto game, he attacked and demolished the front end of the Maple Leaf Gardens Zamboni; he later paid the $500 repair bill the Leafs sent him—Samuelsson has now brought his hard but steadying skills to the Rangers' blue line. On the Swedish national team, the Tre Kronor coaches have more or less shunned him over the years, but he remains a fan favorite. "He's very popular in Sweden," says Samuelsson's 20-year-old countryman and Ranger teammate, Niklas Sundstrom. "We've got more guys going over to the tough play because they see that he's doing so well here."

A Swedish national team stocked with players like Samuelsson? No egg would stand a chance.

*PRESS YOUR LUCK-Going into the Rangers' zone with Ulf Samuelsson on defense is a tricky proposition.*

# Mats Sundin

MAPLE LEAF GARDENS, OCTOBER 15, 1995: MATS SUNDIN HAMMERS HOME THE FIRST OF A PAIR OF GOALS in a stellar four-point night against the visiting Islanders. More than the usual quiet smile crosses his face, pretty as a Swedish pop star's: Sundin's in a frenzy, roaring above the jubilation of the Toronto crowd, wheeling behind the Isles' net and pounding the glass with his fist in a weird mix of fury and triumph totally out of character for him. ● Yet it made perfect sense. ● Most fans would be delighted if their team traded away a player who in nine years had only twice managed more than 45 points in a season and missed more than 4 out of every 11 games to injury, and in return received a 23-year-old budding superstar who had averaged nearly 84 points a season and missed just four games in four years. ● Some fans, however, would lament the player dealt away and resent rather than embrace the player acquired. They did in Toronto, where the departed player was Wendel Clark, the often-brutish, often-injured, but beloved inspirational sparkplug of the Leafs, and the player acquired was Sundin, big, graceful, and immensely skilled, but somehow unproven and, well, Swedish. ● The occasion of Sundin's outburst was Clark's first Gardens appearance since he'd been traded to Quebec for Sundin more than a year earlier, and had since been moved to the Islanders. The Hogtown faithful were effusive in welcoming Clark back into the old building. So Sundin's exhibition was a *cri de coeur* for the acceptance he hadn't felt, in spite of having led the Leafs in scoring in his first season with the club and having turned in a superb 10-point playoff performance as the Leafs lost a seven-game opening-round heartbreaker to Chicago. ● Sundin, as a youngster growing up in the Stockholm suburbs, had idolized countryman Borje Salming, the great trail-blazing defenseman of the '70s and '80s Leafs. Sundin's numbers in Swedish junior weren't impressive, but the tall, wiry teen showed enough skill for Quebec to make him the first pick in the 1989 Entry Draft—the first European ever chosen first overall. ● He bagged his first NHL goal in his first game, and his rookie campaign was a respectable one, with 23 goals and 59 points for a Nordiques' team that was loading up with young talent but had yet to jell. Sundin's brightest moments came in that spring's World Championships. With the score tied 1-1 in the third period of the gold-medal game against the Soviet Union, Sundin burst in one-on-one against Slava Fetisov, the great Russian blueliner, turned him into a pretzel, and scored the tournament-winning goal.

His shaky confidence boosted, and having beefed up his 6-4 frame to 215 pounds, Sundin went on the attack as an NHL sophomore, striking for 33 goals and 76 points and rolling up 103 penalty minutes with a more aggressive game. His long strides already gave him deceptive speed, and his size, augmented by the longest sticks the NHL allows, made his reach dangerous from anywhere near the crease or behind the net. His added strength enabled him to push logjams of players along the boards and dig out the puck for a wrist shot, slap shot, or backhander, all equally hard and accurate.

All those skills came together in Sundin's third season. Coming off a nine-points-in-nine-games showing in Prague, where Sweden repeated as world champions, he began 1992-93 with a 30-game point-scoring streak. The explosion propelled Sundin to 47 goals, 114 points, and a fine plus-21 mark, and Les Nordiques back to the playoffs for the first time in six years. It all came to an abrupt end, however, as eventual Cup-champion Montreal knocked off their inexperienced provincial archrivals in the opening round.

He came on like gangbusters in '93-94; after 29 games, he was on pace for a 50-goal year. But his tenuous confidence was shaken by the Nords' refusal to upgrade his contract, and he went out like a Dustbuster, with a puny six markers in the season's last 55 games. He still led the team with 32 goals but Quebec sank back out of the playoffs.

S undin will be at the very top level of players in this league. I'm talking elite, the very few right at the peak.

Sundin turned in another great performance at the 1994 World Championships in Milan, leading all tournament scorers with 14 points in nine games, but the Swedes had to settle for bronze, and while working at Salming's hockey school back in Sweden that summer, Sundin learned he had been traded to Toronto.

"Mats had to be apprehensive coming here and replacing Wendel, a guy who was an institution here," said Leafs general manager Cliff Fletcher. "But he handled everything with unbelievable maturity."

"Mats brings a lot of talent to the table," said Leafs captain Doug Gilmour. "He can play defensively, he can play offensively, and he's a guy who, when he's on the ice, he's very graceful on the attack. He's a big man, he's very competitive, and I guess there may be a knock against certain European players, but Mats isn't one of those guys because he goes through the wall for you."

When the 1994-95 season finally got under way, Sundin produced consistently from both wings as well as his natural center position, leading the Leafs in goals and points.

Despite the disappointment of the '95 playoffs, coach Pat Burns saw better things to come. "Sundin will be at the very top level of players in this league," he promised. "I'm talking elite, the very few right at the peak—if he wants to be. It's all there for him to be a dominant player. We have seen only a percentage of what's in that body."

The early-season show against Clark and the Isles was part of it, and Sundin's resilience,

after tearing knee cartilage two weeks later and missing just four games, was more. He bounced back with a 33-goal season in which he led Toronto in assists, points, and plus-minus. A midseason coaching change didn't improve the rest of a slow, aging club, however: Toronto again exited the playoffs in the first round, and Sundin was left to ponder what it means to be a Maple Leaf.

"I know this is a club with history," says the ever quiet and modest Sundin. "It's great to play in a city where hockey means so much, and it's great to have a chance to be part of that history."

Sundin says, "I can only do my best. I'm going to try to convince them that I belong. But I can only hope I'll be like those players on the wall. It would be a great thing, a great honor to hang with those guys. I don't know. I just want to do my job—that comes first.

"If I deserve it, maybe one day they'll hang me up there, too."

*IF LOOKS COULD KILL-Toronto's Mats Sundin would have a goal.*

# Teemu Selanne

WHEREVER TEEMU SELANNE HAS TAKEN HIS RECORD-SHATTERING TALENT, HE HAS IMPRESSED PLAYERS, journalists, and fans with his flash on the rink and his warmth off it. He has thrived in both hemispheres as hockey star and local hero, idolized from Helsinki to Winnipeg to Anaheim. ● Born in the Finnish capital in 1970, Selanne grew up playing hockey and soccer. At age 17 he scored at a two-points-per-game clip with Jokerit's junior team—a performance the Winnipeg Jets found admirable enough to make him their No. 1 draft choice. But Selanne stayed in Finland. The next year, he repeated the two-points-per-game feat and helped the Jokerit senior team win promotion to the first division. Selanne continued to light the lamp time and time again over the next three seasons, including a league-leading 39 goals in 44 games in '91-92. His final numbers in a little over four seasons of Finnish senior-level competition, including time off for military service: 112 goals and 90 assists in 136 regular-season games, and an incredible 17 goals and 10 assists in 15 playoff games. ● Clearly, Selanne was already on a roll when he came to Winnipeg for '92-93 as a 22-year-old NHL rookie. And the change in surroundings—new teammates, a narrower rink, a much longer schedule, more travel, more physical play, not to mention a new language and culture—did nothing to slow him down. Nothing phased him, not even the climate in Winnipeg, which apparently was even more wintry than Helsinki's. "It was colder than I thought," he said. "That was too much. I like snow and I like winter but it was a little bit too cold to enjoy it." ● NHL goalies that year were no match for even a slightly chilled Selanne. On October 14 he registered his first hat trick. On March 2, he tallied his 54th goal, shattering Mike Bossy's 16-year-old rookie goal-scoring record. On March 23, he notched his 110th point to surpass Peter Stastny's 13-year-old rookie point-scoring mark. When the season finally ended, Selanne had scored an incredible 76 goals and 56 assists in 84 games. The speedster with the seeing-eye snap shot had not only outdistanced all rookies and became a shoo-in for the Calder Trophy, he also tied for the league lead among all players in goal-scoring and tied for fifth in overall scoring. In the postseason, his joy at slotting home Winnipeg's first-ever hat trick in the NHL playoffs was dampened when the Jets were eliminated in the first round. But Selanne's phenomenal year was capped when he became the only rookie ever voted to the NHL's First All-Star Team at right wing. ● As acclaimed as he was in North America, he was virtually deified back in Finland, where his games were televised and drew huge ratings. One zealous Finnish journalist called Selanne "the god of

Winnipeg." "I think that's a little bit too much," replied the modest winger. "In Finland we don't have so many sports stars, but hockey is such a big thing now. So if you are a good player, you have a lot of fans. The pressures can be really big, sometimes too big."

Selanne's rookie year was an impossible act to follow. By Christmas the Flying Finn was on pace to score about 45 goals for the season—a fine total for any other second-year man, but apparently not for someone who had scored 76 in his first year. Winnipeg management actually started to publicly question Selanne's commitment; the general manager accused him of being in "dreamland." Any chance of picking up the pace ended in Anaheim in the 51st game of the campaign, when Selanne suffered a 75 percent severed Achilles tendon. His season was finished after 25 goals and 29 assists.

With the '94-95 season delayed, he delighted Jokerit fans—and testing his rehabbed Achilles tendon—by tallying 19 points in 20 games for his old club. But a new injury arose when he returned to Winnipeg for the NHL season: tendinitis in both knees, which Selanne called "a very painful injury. I couldn't push down on my knees at all." He managed a good but somewhat disappointing 48 points in 45 games. He also took only one penalty all season long, a minor, but it was for a two-handed slash on Toronto defenseman Dmitri Mironov that NHL Senior Vice President Brian Burke, in suspending Selanne for two games, called an "unacceptable" act. That episode was an aberration for the 6-foot, 200-pounder, who can check ruggedly but does so while taking remarkably few penalties. Nevertheless, Selanne

®️ & ©️ Mighty Ducks

In Finland we don't have so many sports stars, so the pressures can be really big, sometimes too big.

was still the darling of Jets fans.

In 1995–96, Selanne, healthy for the first time in a year and a half, led the Jets in scoring and was selected for the midseason All-Star Game for the third straight time. Paul Kariya, the young Mighty Ducks star, was Selanne's teammate on the Western Conference side. Afterward, reports Ducks general manager Jack Ferreira, "Paul came back from the All-Star Game and all he could talk about was Teemu." Says Kariya, "I did come back and tell Jack what a great guy Teemu was. He's just real humble and down to earth. It is so rare to see a guy of his stature relate to young players so well."

A few days later, Ferreira acquired Selanne from Winnipeg in exchange for Chad Kilger and Oleg Tverdovsky, the Ducks' past two No. 1 draft choices. When Selanne heard about the trade, he was upset, angrily tearing the nameplate off his Jets locker, but he soon warmed to the idea of playing with the up-and-coming Ducks. He and Kariya were unstoppable, transforming a power play that had been the worst in the league for three years running into a fearsome engine of destruction.

"I can't wait to get to the rink every day," said Anaheim coach Ron Wilson. "You're talking about two of the truly breathtaking talents in the National Hockey League with Paul and Teemu." Selanne's presence energized the Ducks, whose 17-9-3 post-trade record lifted them from the cellar regions to within a single point of the final playoff berth, which was occupied, ironically, by Winnipeg. The Finnish Flash provided the spark, logging 16 goals and 36 points in that span, and finished the season with 40 goals and 108 points,

tied for seventh in the league. Selanne's return to the top echelon of NHL players was complete.

His seasons in the wilderness behind him, Selanne looked forward to playing again for Finland (he'd already represented his country at the '89 World Junior Championships, '91 Canada Cup and World Championships, and the '92 Olympics) and for the Mighty Ducks. "This team has a lot of young, hungry players," said Selanne. "I'm very excited."

So is every hockey fan who watches him perform on the ice.

*ONE MIGHTY DUCK-Anaheim's Teemu Selanne is as dangerous an offensive player as there is in the NHL.*

# United States

The Miracle on Ice took place way back in 1980, yet it still seems like only yesterday, so resonant was that moment in America's sporting consciousness. A handful of college kids from Massachusetts, Minnesota, and Wisconsin enchanted the nation by beating the mighty Soviets and going on to Olympic gold.

Americans remember those magical nights in Lake Placid for their emotion and patriotism—but there was something more. That triumph marked the moment when U.S. hockey truly arrived, when the hockey boom of the late '60s and '70s—which seeded pro franchises and recreational rinks all over the country—bore fruit in skilled, well-schooled American players. From the moment goalie Jim Craig wrapped himself in the Stars and Stripes amid thundering cries of "USA! USA!" Americans would never lag on the ice again.

Hockey has a long and proud history in the U.S., stretching back to the turn of the century, when touring Canadian teams popularized the sport in Boston, New York, and Michigan. The first professional hockey league ever, the International Pro League of 1904-1907, was an all-U.S. affair, with franchises in Pittsburgh and Michigan's Upper Peninsula. Meanwhile, collegiate hockey became a fixture in the Northeast, producing the likes of Hobey Baker, Princeton's legendary six-sport athlete and namesake of college hockey's MVP award. And Frank and Lester Patrick's PCHL included teams in the Pacific Northwest. In 1916 the Portland Rosebuds fell to the Montreal Canadiens in the Stanley Cup Final; the next year the Seattle Metropolitans became the first U.S.-based team to win it outright.

The Boston Bruins became the NHL's first U.S.-based club in 1924, followed within two years by the New York Americans, Pittsburgh Pirates, Chicago Blackhawks, Detroit Cougars (later Red Wings), and New York Rangers. Hockey had come to the States to stay—and U.S. players came with it, like Sault Sainte Marie Michigan native Taffy Abel of the Rangers, Harvard product Myles Lane of the Bruins, and well-traveled Massachusetts center-man Carl Voss. Meanwhile, Chicago owner Major Frederic McLaughlin vowed to win the Stanley Cup with an all-American lineup. Sure enough, he did: the '38 Blackhawks iced nine U.S.-born players, not to mention coach Bill Stewart. That same year, Frankie "Mr. Zero" Brimsek of Eveleth, Minnesota, began his Hall of Fame goal-tending career with the Bruins.

But as the NHL settled into the six-team era of the postwar years, Americans pretty much disappeared from big-time hockey. Even in international play, where the U.S. once stood second only to Canada, their prestige was eclipsed by the rising powers in Europe. There was one astounding surprise, though, during the 1960 Olympics, held in Squaw Valley, California, when the Americans won a gold medal after upsetting the formidable Soviets.

After expansion opened up more NHL roster spots in the early '70s, Americans started to filter back in. By 1980, when Olympians like Neal Broten, Mike Ramsey, Ken Morrow, Dave Christian, and Mark Johnson embarked on distinguished pro careers, it became commonplace to see two or three U.S.-born players on each NHL team. By the '90s, one in five NHLers were Americans, their presence remarkable only by their achievements and no longer by the quirk of their nationality. Joe Mullen of New York's Hell's Kitchen neighborhood has had a 1000-point career; Bobby Carpenter, the first American to score 50 goals in a season, evolved into a Stanley Cup–caliber checker; Reed Larson blasted in over 200 goals from the blue line in a 14-year career; Rod Langway played nearly a thousand games as a superb defensive rearguard; Gary Suter and Phil Housley have created scoring from the blue line for over a decade; John Vanbiesbrouck and Tom Barrasso are among the top goalies in the game; Keith Tkachuk and John LeClair are pouring in goals like mad. The list goes on, as you'll see in the following pages.

Today, the U.S. has reclaimed all its old glory—and more. Internationally, it has a second-place finish in the '91 Canada Cup and a bronze medal in the '96 World Championships under its belt and the promise of titles to come. Domestically, the game is burgeoning, with NHL teams thriving in such previously undreamed of locales as Miami, Tampa Bay, Anaheim, San Jose, Dallas, and Phoenix, minor-league teams sprouting all over the South, and kids playing roller hockey and street hockey everywhere you look.

In fact, with so many people catching hockey fever in warm-weather climes, it seems the game really has found its place in the sun. And if that's truly so, then hockey's American future is so bright, you gotta wear shades.

# Chris Chelios

"I DON'T WANT TO GROW UP," SAYS CHRIS CHELIOS. "I'M LIKE A KID. HOCKEY IS A KID'S GAME AND I LOVE TO play hockey." 🏒 Through 13 seasons on defense for the Montreal Canadiens and Chicago Blackhawks, Chelios has been superb, but the kid he often resembled was the playground bully. There's something new in the hard-hitting veteran's game the last couple of years, though. It just might be maturity. 🏒 Chelios, whose sterling defensive play has been overlooked next to his shooting and passing skills, which have in turn been overshadowed by his predilection for on-ice controversy, has finally made a commitment to more disciplined play. He, his team, and hockey can only be better for it. 🏒 Chelios was born and raised on Chicago's South Side, and remains true to its blue-collar character although he moved to San Diego in high school. He hitchhiked to Canada as a teenager to try out for junior hockey and landed with Tier II Moose Jaw, making enough of an impression at that level that Montreal used their fifth pick, the 40th overall, to select him in the 1981 Entry Draft. That fall he moved on to the University of Wisconsin and legendary coach Bob Johnson. After two years with the Badgers, he earned a berth on the U.S. national team and ultimately the '84 Olympic team. Chelios joined the Canadiens for the last dozen games of the 1983-84 season. 🏒 Through all that, he had never posted big numbers in terms of either points or penalty minutes, making his rapid development into a board-rattling playmaker with the Habs all the more surprising. However, says Chelios, "I had great teachers. Maybe they didn't know they were teaching me. I learned from guys like Rick Green, Larry Robinson, and Jacques Laperriere. Laperriere was a great defenseman when he played, and he was an assistant coach when I was at Montreal. 🏒 "When you come from Chicago you're not necessarily going to get great coaching. The most important thing when I got to Montreal was that I listened and I learned." 🏒 Chelios racked up 64 points as a rookie and played in the NHL All-Star Game. Over the next five seasons, both his point and penalty-minute totals grew steadily. He was a vital member of the Habs when they won the Stanley Cup in 1986, and his 73 points, plus-35 mark, and intimidating physical presence in 1988-89 earned him the Norris Trophy as the league's best defenseman and First Team All-Star honors. At 6-1 and 186 pounds, his hyperaggressive style made him seem four inches and 50 pounds bigger on the ice. 🏒 He co-captained

*STAND BY ME–Chicago's Chris Chelios is a marked player any time he gets near the net.*

the team in '89-90 and made a second trip to the All-Star Game, but that summer he was traded to his hometown Blackhawks in exchange for slick scoring star Denis Savard.

While his defensive play remained rock-solid and his heavy shot from the right point continued to produce offense, his penchant for the bone-crunching check you remember for a long time, the extra shove after the whistle, and the ensuing fights, only increased. He was spending too much time in the penalty box. "Chris's style has worked for and against the team," said Darryl Sutter, then coach of the Blackhawks.

"I was a real pain my first eight or ten years in the league," Chelios concedes. "I liked going out there and being the guy people hate to play against. If I got a chance to get under their skin I would. I thought I was more effective being mean and getting at their top players."

Although Chelios was an annual fixture at the All-Star Game, and even received a second Norris Trophy in 1993, his penalty totals continued to increase—to 282 in '92-93—as he played a more aggressive game. Vowing to get his game under control, before the '93-94 season he promised a friend he would go the whole season without a misconduct penalty. But he was hit with one right away. Against Florida, in Chicago's fifth game of the season, Chelios drew three misconducts, setting a club record with 51 minutes in penalties, and earning a four-game suspension.

Midway through the season, the league sat Chelios down for another four games after a serious fight. He at last began to mend his ways in earnest. "The suspension is maybe what it took for me to learn the hard way," he says. "When something like that happens, it's embarrassing. I'm going to play aggressive and try to be as mean as I can, but I'm going to have to find a line between being mean and taking penalties. That's the biggest commitment I've made and I'm going to do it. If it kills me I'm going to do it."

The Blackhawks' captain did rein in his reckless aggressiveness in the 1994-95 campaign. Jari Kurri noticed the difference. "He's not there pushing you around, yapping, putting a glove in your face," he said. "He's concentrating on his game."

Still tough, coldly efficient, and logging enormous amounts of ice time, Chelios's 1995-96 penalty minutes were half of what they had been just three years earlier, while

He's great leader. Whatever trait or talent a player could have — Chris has it.

he led Chicago in scoring with 72 points and was once again among the NHL's plus-minus leaders. At the end of the '96 season, he had won his third Norris Trophy.

"He's just as important to us as Lemieux or Messier," said Craig Hartsburg, now coach of the Blackhawks. "There are probably three or four players in the league as important to their team as Chelios is to us. When he steps up his game, we step up as a team."

Anaheim star Paul Kariya concurred. "Chelios is the best defenseman in the league," he said. "He gives no gap. When you're going forward, most defensemen go back, but it seems like he's going forward and back at the same time. There's always pressure on the puck."

The Blackhawks' last Stanley Cup triumph came in 1961, almost a year before Chelios was born. For Chelios, now 34, the Cup is "my only goal left in hockey. It has been a long time for Chicago. The fans here deserve it.

"I know everybody says it, but I have that dream I don't know how many times a week. Bringing the Cup down Madison Street—I could quit if that happened.

"When it comes down to it, winning is more important than getting even."

# Brett Hull

FATHERS AND SONS. YOU SEE IT SO OFTEN IN HOCKEY. NO OTHER SPORT HAS SO RICH A LEGACY OF FATHERS and sons playing not just at a major-league level, but achieving All-Star or even Hall of Fame status together—Gordie and Mark Howe, three generations of the Patrick clan, and dozens more. But no father and son have performed more spectacularly than Bobby and Brett Hull. Bobby, the Golden Jet, cannonballed his way through both the NHL and the World Hockey Association from 1957 to 1980 on the left wing; in his prime, he was the fastest-skating, hardest-shooting player in hockey, one of the game's most sensational performers ever. Today his son, the Golden Brett, stylistically his father's opposite in so many ways, even to the point of being a right winger but similarly blond, handsome, and husky, is likewise among the most feared and respected goal-scorers in hockey. "Brett, in on a goaltender, can slow it down to a walk," the elder Hull says of his son. "I went in and blasted away, never looked at the goaltender's feet, or made any in-depth studies. Brett waits and waits, the goaltender puts his weight on one skate, and boom, it's over—buried past the pad he for a second couldn't move." "Maybe I've got his genes," the younger Hull says of his father, "but I definitely don't have his personality. You're talking to the laziest man alive. I'm not into expending physical energy. I'm into expending mental energy. "On the ice, my dad was like a thoroughbred. I'm more like a train. I chug." "People rip him for being a bad skater, but put a puck in front of him and suddenly there's no skater in the universe who can go get it quicker," says Adam Oates, Boston's superb playmaker who centered in St. Louis for Hull's three greatest seasons. "He's got goalies so intimidated that they do the stupidest things. Guys try so hard to figure out how to stop him, they don't do what they normally would. It's really almost pathetic." Brett Hull—intelligent, witty, unabashedly outspoken—was a late bloomer. He went from the rec leagues as a teen to Tier II junior to the University of Minnesota at Duluth, where he terrorized Western Collegiate goalies, piling up 52 goals in 42 games and a WCHA First All-Star team berth in 1985-86. It was there that the chunky young forward, born in Winnipeg, raised there and in Vancouver, chose to play internationally for his adopted homeland, the United States. Hull was the first to admit to being a one-dimensional player when he started out in the NHL, and Calgary management took the overly modest youngster at his word. Despite a 50-goal, AHL rookie-of-the-year campaign for Moncton in 1986-87, and 26 goals in 52 games with the big club the following season, the Flames traded the budding superstar to St. Louis in March 1988.

"What I find amazing is that he went from nothing to star faster than anyone I've ever heard of," says Oates. "With Gretzky, people understood the guy was going to be great from the time he was fifteen. Brett went from nothing to god in what amounts to an instant."

Hull produced 41 goals in his first full year with the Blues, then, teamed with Oates, turned in three of the greatest goal-scoring seasons in hockey history—72 goals in 1989-90, 86 in his '90-91 Hart Trophy campaign, and another 70-goal outing in 1991-92. Equally incredible were the 28 times he scored in 31 playoff games over those three years. He earned NHL First Team All-Star honors in 1990 and '91.

"Sure, he shoots the puck a zillion miles an hour, and maybe his slap shot is nastier than his dad's, harder than there has ever been," says Florida netminder John Vanbiesbrouck. "But let's get real. Brett Hull's shot is all about release."

As admirable as his quick trigger and thunderbolt shot is Hull's pacific approach to the game. He earned the Lady Byng Trophy for gentlemanly play in 1990, was runner-up in '91, and remains an annual contender. "I'm not going to fight anyone," Hull declares proudly. "When I chase defensemen into the corner in the course of a game, I'm telling them I'm behind them and to move it. I don't want to hurt anyone."

Hull's maturation as a two-way player has many times been overlooked. For example, he has finished six of his eight years playing for the Blues in the upper echelon of the team's plus/minus charts. He has excelled in international play, whether with the United States

> When I chase defensemen into the corner, I'm telling them I'm behind them and to move it.

team at the World Championships or in the old Canada Cup.

"There's no question Brett has developed into one of the most dominant forces in the game at both ends of the rink," says former Blues assistant coach Ted Sator, citing his success in checking, passing, and penalty-killing. "He's committed to team success. He has conformed."

Conforming seems like the least likely avenue Hull would ever take. "I love controversy," he admits with a ready laugh. "Heck, even I don't believe half of what I say."

Hull's laid-back attitude, and his almost mystical concept of his role on the ice, have helped give him a reputation as hockey's hippie. He has been known to sing happily to himself out on the ice in crucial situations. "High-strung is not what I would call him," says Oates.

"I believe that when you are most out of the play, you are the furthest in it," says Hull. "My whole game, in fact, is based on deception. I'm there, and then I'm not. I don't do a lot because I don't want to be noticed. I don't want to be seen. I barely raise my arms when I score. I don't want people mad at me for making them look stupid.

"My brain thinks totally opposite to everyone else. I take the step looking for the goal, and that may mean the step is this way when everyone else is going that way. I have an unbelievably vivid imagination.

"There comes that moment when I have lost myself and only the play finds me. And I have nothing but confidence in my ability to bury the puck in the net at that moment."

Hull produced two more seasons of 50-plus goals in 1992-93 and '93-94, and his 64 tallies in

92 career playoff games represent a pace exceeded only by Mario Lemieux.

Having scored more times than any other NHL player in the last eight years, having set 42 St. Louis scoring records, having won some of hockey's highest awards, only one objective has eluded the happy-go-lucky goal-scoring machine.

"People can say you're a superstar or whatever they want to call you," Hull says, "but you never really feel like one until you become part of the Stanley Cup. That's the one thing I have to get before my career is over. To me the regular season is all for contract and for the awards and all that, but playoffs prove what kind of player you really are."

Whether or not the postseason is ever as kind to him as it justly should be, Brett Hull has already proven what kind of player he is—one of the most entertaining, refreshingly candid, and, for all his lighthearted insouciance, relentlessly goal-hungry men ever to play this great game.

*MAD ABOUT YOU-You can grab him, hook him, and hug him, but St. Louis's Brett Hull usually is able to maintain control of the puck.*

# Pat LaFontaine

BACK IN THE GOLDEN AGE OF RADIO, ONE OF THE MOST POPULAR SHOWS WAS "JACK ARMSTRONG, THE All-American Boy," which featured the adventures of a fictional college athlete. Jack was not only the most talented performer on his team, but also the bravest, smartest, kindest, most handsome, most modest, most gentlemanly young man in all of sport. Pure fantasy then, even in a seemingly long-gone era of clean-cut, well-spoken, well-behaved athletes? No, in fact, it's time for an updated true-life version: "Pat LaFontaine, the All-American Boy." Our story opens in the American heartland, St. Louis, Missouri, where LaFontaine was born in 1965. Still a boy, he moved with his family to the Detroit suburb of Waterford, where his father taught LaFontaine and his brother and sister to skate on frozen Williams Lake. At 16, he caught the attention of scouts with a 175-goal, 300-point season in midget for Detroit Compuware. The following season, LaFontaine went to Canada to test his talents against major junior competition. He was a phenomenon. In his only season of junior play, LaFontaine rang up amazing totals—104 goals, 130 assists, 234 points—earning awards as Quebec Junior League and Canadian Junior Player of the Year, and topping all playoff scorers with 35 points in just 15 playoff games as he led Verdun Junior Canadiens to the Memorial Cup. He even learned some French during his year in Quebec, endearing himself to the province's fans while getting closer to his family's French-Canadian roots. The Stanley Cup champion New York Islanders made him their first choice, the third player selected, in the 1983 Entry Draft. Only his relatively small size—something less than his listed 5-10 and 180 pounds—kept him from going first overall. The 1984 Olympics, though, were LaFontaine's next challenge. Touring with the U.S. national team, he averaged nearly a goal and an assist per game through 58 pre-Olympic matches. And although the club flopped in their mission to duplicate the gold-medal miracle of the 1980 U.S. team, LaFontaine was superb, scoring five goals and five assists without a penalty minute in six Olympic contests. He joined the Islanders for the end of the 1983-84 season, and promptly ripped 13 goals in just 15 games. He had come to the team at the end of its four-year Cup dynasty, but although the club aged and dwindled over the next several seasons, LaFontaine inproved by the year. A 54-point rookie campaign was followed by a 30-goal sophomore season, and then a 38-goal effort in 1986-87. That season's playoffs provided one of the most memorable moments in LaFontaine's career and in Cup history: the Easter Epic, a white-knuckle, four-overtime, opening-round, Game 7 marathon in Washington. After three

regulation periods, three full scoreless overtimes, and eight and a half minutes of a fourth, the Caps and Isles were tied 2-2 when LaFontaine garnered a rebound, wheeled, and fired a spinnerama slapper off the left post for a dramatic win. His accurate blast ended the longest NHL game in 44 years, and completed the Isles' comeback from a 3 games to 1 deficit in the series.

The following season was the first of six consecutive 40-goal campaigns, which elevated LaFontaine to the level of the NHL's elite forwards. The centerman's best Islander campaign came in 1989-90, when he notched a splendid 54 goals and 105 points. By then LaFontaine was recognized as one of the most exciting and inspirational players in hockey. His breakaway speed let him take full advantage of his ability to find open ice, and his astonishing lateral quickness let him elude checks in the middle of the rink or deep in the corners.

The epitome of a LaFontaine rush sees him bursting through the neutral zone near the right boards, bearing down on a lone rearguard and curling past him with a crossover step, leaning back into the defender with his left shoulder and protecting the puck with his body until he cuts across the low slot and snaps the puck over a sprawling netminder. Acceleration, a low center of gravity, and tremendous balance are three key elements of that kind of play, but a fourth is LaFontaine's obsessive attention to his skates. He takes meticulous care with every detail—he prefers an unusually flat blade, tailoring the hollow of the blade for different rinks and sharpening them between periods of games.

A 41-goal year in '90-91 was to be his last on

LaFontaine was recognized as one of the most exciting and inspirational players in hockey.

the Island; after the season, he was traded to Buffalo for the young center Pierre Turgeon. The Sabres, a club that had not won a playoff series in nine years, had accumulated a fair amount of talent but suffered from "a lack of character," as John Muckler, who had taken over as coach and general manager, put it. "That's why we made certain trades, and the first trade we made was to get Pat LaFontaine." And the sweater they gave him was the one with the "C."

Buffalo fans were wowed by LaFontaine both on and off the ice and immediately took him to their collective bosom. When he was felled by a serious jaw injury at midseason it was regarded as the greatest local calamity since the steel mills closed. But he returned ahead of schedule and finished with superb numbers—46 goals and 47 assists in only 57 games.

In '92-93 LaFontaine and the young Russian winger Alexander Mogilny combined to produce scoring totals of historic proportions. Although LaFontaine is a right-handed shot and Mogilny played right wing. Mogilny filled the nets with 76 goals, mostly off passes from LaFontaine, who wired home 53 goals of his own and added 95 assists as he rang up an enormous 148 points. LaFontaine then led Buffalo to their first playoff win since 1983, as the Sabres eliminated Boston. But the price was exorbitant: LaFontaine suffered a severe knee injury. He struggled on bravely, but only aggravated the ligament damage as Sabres succumbed in the next round.

Two lost seasons followed as LaFontaine's injury defied rehab and surgery. He forced his way onto the ice in only 38 games in 1993-94 and '94-95 combined, although, even hobbled, he produced

45 points, and was awarded the Masterton Trophy for his comeback efforts in 1995.

LaFontaine was at last healthy to start in 1995-96, but in his absence such high-scoring teammates as 50-goal man Alexander Mogilny had been traded. Yet, LaFontaine carried on with uncommon class and exceptional success.

"If you look at the other superstars in the league, they have superstars to play with," admits Sabres' coach, Ted Nolan. "It's no discredit to the guys he's playing with, but he has really elevated his play and elevated the play of our team." Despite the absence of a supporting cast, LaFontaine rolled up 40 goals and 51 assists in '95-96, including the 900th point of his career.

The Sabre captain and articulate ambassador for the game reflected on his public accessibility and busy charity work. "I think there's a certain responsibility that goes along with being an athlete," he said. "It's a relatively short career, 10 or 15 years. But it's a perfect opportunity to help those less fortunate. Let's be honest, I feel very fortunate that I've been blessed with a talent and play a game I love. There are children born every day that don't have that opportunity. I'm just a big believer in counting your blessings and trying to give back as much as you can."

The Sabres, and hockey, couldn't ask for any more.

*WHICH WAY DID HE GO?-Buffalo's Pat LaFontaine is zigging and zagging, and the Whalers are dropping.*

# Brian Leetch

THE UNITED STATES HAS PRODUCED A SURPRISING NUMBER OF MARQUEE DEFENSEMEN OVER THE LAST 20 years—Rod Langway, Mark Howe, Chris Chelios, Gary Suter, Phil Housley, Kevin Hatcher, to name but a few— but only one has consistently been compared to Canada's Ray Bourque, the greatest all-around rearguard of the current era. That defenseman is Brian Leetch of the Rangers, one of only three Americans ever to win the Norris Trophy as the league's best blueliner, and the only American ever to win the Conn Smythe Trophy as playoff MVP. How Leetch actually measures up to Bourque's lofty standards is a question best left unanswered for another 10 years or so, when Leetch's full career can be assessed against that of the great Bruin. But one thing is for certain right now: Brian Leetch is a dominant, electrifying, game-breaking defenseman; every time he steps on the ice, he is a threat to make a play of mind-bending imagination and creativity. Quiet, even-tempered, modest to a fault, Leetch lets his actions on the ice do his talking for him. And they say plenty. Like in Game 7 of the tension-drenched 1994 semifinals against the Devils at Madison Square Garden. The score was 0–0 in the game's 30th minute when Leetch tried to go deep behind the Devils' net, but upon reaching the corner found his way blocked by Devil Bill Guerin. So he stopped on a dime and, spinning counterclockwise with the puck on his backhand, twirled away from Guerin to the lip of the goal crease, completing his 360-degree pirouette by slamming the puck between Martin Brodeur's pads and into the net. His actions spoke again in Game 7 of the Cup Final, when he drifted in unchecked to the left of Vancouver goalie Kirk McLean, took a seeing-eye pass from defense partner Sergei Zubov, and fired in one swift motion, giving New York a 1–0 lead it would never relinquish. Later that night, Leetch– whose 34 points made him the playoffs' leading scorer and who had been on ice for 61 of the Blueshirts' 81 post-season goals—would hoist both the Stanley Cup and the Conn Smythe. Bill Clinton reached him by phone follow-ing the game and told him, "Congratulations, man." Deadpanned Leetch, after thanking the president and concluding a short conversation: "Was that Dana Carvey?" Leetch has been a game-breaker since his childhood in Connecticut. His father, who had played both forward and defense in his college days with Boston College, groomed Leetch for a career on the blue line by teaching him how to skate backward before he taught him how to skate forward. John Gardner, his coach at Avon Old Farms prep school, remembers Leetch's first scrim-mage. "He went in, faked the defenseman out, faked the goalie out, and just skated away. All the kids

*LIVING ON THE EDGE—Rangers defenseman Brian Leetch uses his upper body strength to get around Chicago's Cam Russell while Eric Daze looks on.*

started looking at each other. They're all going, 'Wow, holy moley, look at that play!' From then on, whenever Leetch got the puck, the kids would stand up to watch him. They knew he was something special." After leading Avon Old Farms to an undefeated season his senior year,

the team fell behind 6–0 in the New England prep school's final against Jeremy Roenick and Tony Amonte's Thayer Academy. Playing with a badly sprained wrist, Leetch scored twice to lead a furious comeback—but a futile one, as Avon lost, 6–4. That summer the Rangers made Leetch their first draft choice, one of the few American high schoolers ever to go in the first round.

Leetch's next stop was his father's alma mater, Boston College. He promptly led B.C. to the Hockey East title, earned All-America honors, and became the first freshman ever to be nominated for the Hobey Baker Award. He left school to captain the '88 U.S. Olympic team, and later joined the Rangers, scoring an impressive 14 points in 17 games. The next year he won the Calder Trophy with 23 goals in 68 games, still a record for rookie defensemen. He was already showing signs of the dazzling talent that would prompt his teammate, goalie Mike Richter, to marvel, "He's a defensive version of Gretzky."

In '91–92 Leetch won the Norris Trophy with a 102-point campaign (which made him only the fifth defenseman, after Bobby Orr, Paul Coffey, Denis Potvin, and Al MacInnis, to reach the century mark in one season) and sparked the Rangers to first place overall for the first time in 50 years. But that impressive achievement was soon forgotten in the aftermath of yet another early Ranger playoff exit. More disappointment followed for Leetch in '93. He suffered a damaged nerve in his neck and right shoulder, keeping him out of 34 games. Nine days after he returned to action, he got out of a cab near his home on Manhattan's West Side late at night, slipped on an icy patch, and fractured his right ankle, finishing him for the season. Without Leetch, the Rangers plummeted to last place in their division and missed the playoffs.

Coming off that disaster, Leetch decided to do something he hadn't done much of before—build up his body in the off-season. But new Ranger

They're all going, 'Wow, holey moley, look at that play!' From then on the kids would stand up and watch him.

coach Mike Keenan challenged Leetch to build up his endurance still further—and to pay more attention to matters in his own end. "You're no Chris Chelios the way you're playing," Keenan is reported to have told Leetch. "If you're going to be a leader on this team, you've got to accept the responsibility of playing like one." Whether he agreed with the criticism or not, Leetch quietly accepted it, then responded with an MVP-caliber postseason. "When Brian speaks in the locker room, everybody listens," says Colin Campbell, who succeeded Keenan as Rangers coach. "How often does he say something? Every seven or eight months."

After a modest (by his standards) 1995, Leetch led the NHL in defenseman scoring in '95–96, and once again keyed a Ranger power play that has annually been one of the league's best since he joined the team. Meanwhile, the argument continues among those who insist on comparing Leetch to Bourque. "Get it out of your mind," Boston general manager Harry Sinden insisted when asked the question in '95. "That is a comparison that never should be made." The ever-modest Leetch agreed. "Ray Bourque has been at the top of his position since he came into the league," he said. "It's unfair to compare me to him. It upset my relatives in Boston more than me." Meanwhile, Leetch's teammate Mark Messier responded to Sinden thus: "All I know is we got a banner hanging up there."

That much is true. And it's up there not because Brian Leetch plays like Bourque or Chelios or any other defenseman, but because he plays like Brian Leetch.

CRASH LANDING-
*New York Rangers defense-
man Brian Leetch prepares
to hit the ice but is still able
to keep both eyes on the play
in front of him.*

# Mike Modano

IN THE WORLD OF HOCKEY, NO OUTPOST IS SO REMOTE AS DALLAS, TEXAS. THAT DOESN'T MEAN THAT someday soon it won't be as well integrated into the discourse of the game as such once-faraway locales as Moscow, Prague, or Los Angeles. But for now Dallas seems to lie at the very end of the earth, in the vaguest, farthest reaches of hockey's imagination. 🏒 You'd think, therefore, that a player who grew up in the very heartland of the game—someone born and raised just outside Detroit, who matured on the Saskatchewan prairie, who turned pro in Minnesota—would be less than thrilled about playing in a place as far removed as Dallas. But not Mike Modano, the swift-skating centerman of the Dallas Stars. The Big D—its climate, its wealth, the way it heaps adoration on its star athletes—suits him just fine. "I love it down here," says Modano. 🏒 Surely Modano had no idea he'd end up there, back when he was first introduced to hockey in his hometown of Livonia, Michigan, at age 9. According to his mother, young Mike was an "extremely rough" boy, so she and his father tried to channel his energies into the most vigorous sport around. At first he balked, but his natural athletic abilities (at 8 he had won the Michigan Punt, Pass & Kick football skills contest) won out, and soon Mike was playing round the clock. Like so many future NHLers, he played hour after hour in his basement and driveway, slamming the puck against a wall, or, in winter, skating on a rink in his flooded backyard. 🏒 After lighting up the competitive Detroit youth hockey circuit, Modano, a skinny 16-year-old with braces on his teeth, made the big leap to Canadian major junior play, joining the Prince Albert Raiders of the Western Hockey League. "He looked like he was about 14," remembers Rick Wilson, his Raiders coach. "He came to our town and I thought, 'Cripes, he's going to die.'" 🏒 But instead of dying, the quiet, unknown kid from Detroit went on to tally 62 points in 70 games. In his second year he skyrocket-ed to 127 points in 65 games—development dramatic enough to prompt the Minnesota North Stars to make Modano, four days past his 18th birthday, the first player chosen in the '88 draft. He celebrated his good fortune by leaving the draft meeting in Montreal to fly back to Prince Albert for his senior prom. 🏒 Modano played one more year of junior, collecting 105 points in just 41 games, before joining the North Stars for two playoff games in '89. He started his NHL career in earnest in '89-90, yet such were the burdens of being the No. 1 pick that some already doubted his character. "The Detroit players were quoted as saying he was the most overrated player in the league," recalls Stars assistant general manager Doug Armstrong. Modano was "overrated" enough to score 29 goals and 75 points in 80 games, and he finished second to Soviet Elite League veteran Sergei Makarov in the Calder Trophy voting.

In Modano's second year the North Stars posted a miserable 27-39-14 record, but went on a roll in the playoffs, knocking off three clubs—including defending Cup-holders Edmonton—to reach the Stanley Cup Final. Those North Stars, the second-worst regular-season team to ever reach the Cup Final, got there thanks to Modano. The 6-3, 190-pounder struck for 16 points in 17 games in the first three rounds. "I remember saying I was happy to be there," says Modano, "but really happy for the older guys like Neal Broten, Brian Bellows, and Bobby Smith because they may not get back there again." Alas, Minnesota went down in six to Pittsburgh. And these many years later, he looks back on the experience with an increasing sense of loss. "Now people are saying I may not get back there again. You don't realize how tough it is to get back there until you're older."

The next two seasons Modano accumulated 170 points in 158 games, but each spring all he had to show for it was a trip to the World Championships with the U.S. national team—the traditional consolation for top American players after their club teams bow out early. Meanwhile, the North Stars moved to Dallas, and suddenly Modano found himself deep in the heart of Texas.

The move agreed with Modano. "Guys with convertibles drive to the rink with the top down, and you can wear shorts to practice," he said during his first winter there. "How could you not like living in Dallas?" Perhaps it was the weather that got the lanky Modano to change his style.

Mike looked like he was about 14. He came to our town and I thought, 'Cripes, he's going to die.'

Where formerly he took his shots from the outside, leading Minnesota fans to deride him as "soft," he now barged into the slot, absorbed punishment, and beat goalies from in close. The result: 50 goals in '93-94, propelling the Stars to a 42-29-13 mark, the club's third-best showing ever. And even though Dallas bowed out in the second round to eventual Finalists Vancouver, the city took the team, and especially Modano, to heart.

In a place that deifies its sports heroes, Modano, an eligible bachelor who favors Armani suits while devoting a substantial amount of his time to community efforts, is the object of a lot of people's affection; he even finds marriage proposals slipped under the windshield wipers of his car. "To the extent that we have a heartthrob player who appeals to the 14-, 15-, and 16-year-olds," says Stars marketing Vice President Bill Strong. "Michael would be it. He looks a little like Tom Cruise, only taller and blonder."

Soon after the shortened '95 campaign got underway, the lone star on the Lone Star team wowed the league with a two-goal, four-assist night against Anaheim. But aside from that performance, he never did regain the touch he had the year before, in part because the Stars' defense-first system keeps a leash on rushing forwards like Modano. With a month to go in the season, he missed four games with a badly bruised right ankle, then hurried back into the lineup to help his struggling team, only to rupture two tendons in his left ankle. Through for the year with 29 points in 30 games, Modano could only look forward to '95-96. But personal totals of 36-45-81 in 78 games, and a dismal team

winning percentage of .402 that left Dallas out of the playoffs, added up to another disappointing season.

"One thing I've always had in the back of my mind is that the Minnesota North Stars drafted me No. 1," says Modano of the nagging sense that he hasn't quite lived up to his potential. "They made a decision that included me in their plans, their future. I felt like I owed a lot to that organization."

Dallas fans can't wait until their heartthrob realizes that huge potential. If you think they adore Modano now . . .

*FOR YOUR EYES ONLY-Dallas's Mike Modano, a 36-goal scorer in 1995-96, has that ready-to-score glare in his eyes as he prepares to pounce on a loose puck.*

# Mike Richter

JUNE 7, 1994. THE PACIFIC COLISEUM, VANCOUVER, BRITISH COLUMBIA. GAME 4 OF THE STANLEY CUP FINAL. Thirteen minutes left in the second period. The Rangers leading the series, 2 games to 1, but losing this contest, 2 goals to 1. The Canucks' Pavel Bure rockets away at center ice on his way to a penalty shot. If he makes it, the Rangers can pretty well kiss this game goodbye, and perhaps the series, too. ⬮ In the Ranger net, Mike Richter watches as Bure picks up speed. It was only four months earlier, during an MVP performance in the NHL All-Star Game, that Richter stopped Bure on four separate breakaways. Just a few minutes before in this game, the Ranger backstop had turned aside six Vancouver shots in one 15-second flurry. But if these memories flicker through Richter's mind as Bure hits the blue line, he is not consciously aware of them. Surely they are present somewhere, along with all the other knowledge stored up over almost two decades of stopping pucks at the pro and amateur level, all brought into play in the instantaneous melding of mind and reflex and muscle that is the special province of the goalie. ⬮ Richter drifts out beyond the lip of the crease in case Bure shoots from the high slot. But Bure keeps coming, so Richter backs in toward the goalmouth. At about eight feet, Bure fakes right, onto his backhand, then draws the puck onto his forehand, then backhand to forehand again as he reaches the top of the crease. Richter goes down into a split, "his legs," in one writer's words, "as far apart as a human male can spread them without shrieking." With Richter's right skate blade kissing the near goalpost, there is simply nothing for Bure to shoot at. At the moment of truth, all he can do as he jets past the left side of the crease is jam the puck into Richter's right pad, then watch it bounce harmlessly away. "It was," said Ranger coach Mike Keenan after the Rangers rallied to steal the game, 4-2, and go up 3 to 1 in a series they would eventually win, "the most important save of Michael's career." ⬮ Critical moments define any great goalie's professional life, but Richter seems to have had more than most. He was brilliant throughout the '94 playoffs, but that save is what most people will talk about 50 years from now. It's a good thing, because until Richter kicked out Bure's penalty shot, he was known for another critical moment—one with an unhappy denouement. With five minutes to go in a '92 quarterfinal game against Pittsburgh, Richter flubbed a routine 75-footer for a late, tide-turning goal that eventually led to the Rangers' elimination. The gaffe haunted Richter—there was even a reprise in a '94 quarterfinal match against the Capitals, when he whiffed on Kevin Hatcher's blooping dump-in—until he finally got to hoist the Stanley Cup on June 14,

*THE ERASER-New York's Mike Richter slides across the net to stop a potential Ottawa Senators' goal.*

1994. Now, of course, he's recognized for what he is: one of the best goaltenders playing the game today.

Mixing the acrobatic daredeviltry of expansion-era Roger Crozier and the Kings' Kelly Hrudey with the brick-wall standup style of vintage Bernie Parent, Richter epitomizes a new breed of goaler—the kind who blends sound positional play and catlike reflexes with the physical flexi-

bility of Plastic Man. Vladislav Tretiak was the first of this breed; Arturs Irbe, at his best, is another incarnation. Richter works hard to achieve the explosive lateral movement and limber agility that is his trademark. His rigorous off-season training includes an hour of daily stretching exercises and several hours of strenuous leg work. But on top of that, Richter also works on his concentration by reading prodigiously. "You can say I visit a mental gymnasium every day," he says. "Reading is bound up with goaltending. Tending goal requires me to remain focused, not distracted. So does reading. I'm convinced that reading makes me a better athlete."

Richter must have been a voracious reader at an early age, because he's been a top goalie since he started playing the position in the suburban Philadelphia youth leagues at age 6. Chosen in the second round of the '85 draft by the Rangers, Richter went on to play two years with the University of Wisconsin, and started four matches for the U.S. team at the 1998 winter Olympics in Calgary. After a year as an IHL regular, Richter debuted with the Rangers in Game 4 of an '89 preliminary-round playoff series they were losing to Pittsburgh, 3 games to none. The 22-year-old performed gamely in a 4–3 loss, but he was in the NHL to stay.

The following year, Richter alternated through 76 straight games with longtime Ranger regular and one-time Vezina Trophy winner John Vanbiesbrouck. That situation held for the next two years as well, but even though it gave the Rangers the best goalkeeping tandem in the game, neither man liked it. Rangers general manager Neil Smith was finally forced to choose prior to the '93–94 expansion draft. He protected Richter, and Vanbiesbrouck wound up with the Florida Panthers. That season, Vanbiesbrouck's herculean work between the pipes single-handedly got the first-year Panthers to within a single point of the playoffs. Richter's efforts got the Rangers the Cup.

Talkative and intelligent, Richter has said he is interested in a career in politics or public service

Tending goal requires me to stay focused. So does reading. I'm convinced that reading makes me a better athlete.

after he hangs up his skates. He has taken summer courses at Cornell and Columbia toward finishing his B.A. in philosophy, but for now his efforts are centered on guarding the nets. "The nature of this position," says the Manhattan-dwelling goalie, "is you have to prove yourself again and again. That's where you get the challenge and that's what makes it fun."

Richter will meet another challenge in the coming years on the revived international stage, where the United States will ice a team some believe will join Canada and Russia at the pinnacle of world hockey. Just getting a place on the U.S. team will be a difficult proposition. Only a handful of American goalkeepers have ever earned regular NHL starting jobs, but it's also true that the best of this small lot, Richter included, are as good as any in the world. The first were Mike Karakas and Hall of Famer Frank Brimsek back in the '30s and '40s, but no American would again appear regularly in an NHL goal until the early '80s, and even since then, only perhaps half a dozen Americans have been No. 1 goalies. Still, any national team coach anywhere would be happy to have to choose from among, say, Richter, Vanbiesbrouck, Pittsburgh's two-time Stanley Cup winner Tom Barrasso, or phenom Jim Carey of the Washington Capitals.

Will that challenge be fun? As much fun as stopping Pavel Bure that critical night in Vancouver? Only time will tell. But as Richter himself says, "Sometimes adversity can be a real measure of what you have inside." If that's true, then Mike Richter, who has endured the kind of on-ice adversity only a goalie can experience and gone on to succeed at the highest level, will be just fine.

*A VIEW FROM ABOVE-New York's Mike Richter can bend in ways most men can't.*

# Jeremy Roenick

ASK BERNIE NICHOLLS, VETERAN CENTER OF THE CHICAGO BLACKHAWKS, ABOUT HIS TEAMMATE JEREMY Roenick, and he'll tell you, "Everybody in the league knows how good he is. He's strong. He's fast. He's creative. He takes the body, and that gets the team going. He may not be the best defensive forward in the league, but he's pretty good. I'm trying to find a weakness in Jeremy Roenick's game, but I don't think he has one." ● Ask any one of his teammates, ask most of the players in the National Hockey League, and they'll tell you pretty much the same thing. ● So will Jeremy Roenick: "The one thing I'm most proud of," Roenick says, "is being that complete player. I don't want to be remembered or known as a player who only plays offense, only plays defense, or is only a fighter or a tough guy. I want to bring as much to the table as possible. ● "What's different about me from other players is I know the game really well. I know what to do or where to be in every situation. I can see where all my players are. So sometimes you don't have to be the fastest out there if you play well position-wise. ● "People get excited when I do things. I bring the fans into the game more than other people do. I throw pucks to the crowd, I high-five people over the glass. I let them know that I appreciate them. In a way I'm a showboat, but I get the job done." ● No brag; just fact. Although most NHLers are uniformly—and genuinely—self-effacing about their skills, Roenick doesn't come off cocky or arrogant by contrast. He's just being his usual candid, straight-shooting self, happy to talk about himself, eager to offer an opinion on any subject. ● "I speak my mind and sometimes maybe I shouldn't, but I do," says Roenick. "I don't want to be a controversial figure. I don't want to be the quotemaster. The team is more important to me." ● And Roenick, as the Blackhawks' go-to guy, has given his all to the team for the last seven seasons. Four 40-goal seasons, two 50-goal years, three 100-point campaigns, consistently high plus/minus marks, four All-Star Game appearances, and five broken noses are evidence of his effort and determination. ● "It's just something in my heart," says the player his fans and teammates simply call "JR." "It's just my will to succeed." ● His accomplishments are all the more impressive considering the route he took to NHL stardom. The Boston-born Roenick grew up in Virginia; as an adolescent, he commuted to play for the New Jersey Rockets, the amateur team for which the Mullen brothers, the legends of Manhattan's Hell's Kitchen, had once played. His family moved back to Boston in order to provide Roenick with a higher level of competition. At 17, he enrolled at Thayer Academy, a tony prep school, where he romped to 34 goals and 84 points in just 24 games. ●

AND THEY'RE OFF-
*Chicago's Jeremy Roenick
collects the puck and is set
to move into the Rangers
zone, as Mark Messier prepares to pursue.*

Still, after the players they hoped to draft were taken, Chicago merely settled for Roenick, the wiry 160-pound American high school kid, with their first pick, the eighth overall, in the 1988 Entry Draft. Then-coach Mike Keenan arranged for Roenick to play for Hull of the Quebec Major Junior League; he surprised by nearly duplicating his prep-school numbers. After a first-team all-star performance for Team USA at the World Junior Championships, Roenick joined the Blackhawks for the last 20 games of the 1988-89

season, scoring 18 points.

Roenick produced a very respectable 66 points in 78 games in his first full campaign, and added a team-leading 11 goals in 20 playoff games before Chicago fell in the 1990 semifinals. But he came into his own in just his second complete season, finishing second on the Blackhawks with 41 goals, 53 assists, and 94 points, leading the club with a sparkling plus-38 rating. Already one of the fastest, shiftiest skaters in hockey and possessing a deadly accurate shot, Roenick had beefed up to almost 200 pounds, enabling him to add a more aggressive physical element to his game.

"If I could play every game with blood on my face, I'd do it," he says. "It's just a mentality, a badge of honor. If people look at me and see blood on my face, see me with a black eye, they say, 'Geez, that guy is tough.' That's important to me, very important.

"I'll try not to fear anything on the ice. You know what my biggest fear is? It's being disliked by my teammates, my peers, the fans, people around me. I have a fear of not succeeding. I don't fear pain. I don't fear people. Not being accepted and not being successful, those are my fears."

Roenick gave himself little to worry about, then, skating with Steve Larmer and Michel Goulet, and notching back-to-back 50-goal, 100-point seasons in 1991-92 and '92-93. In spite of a broken hand, his 12 goals and 22 points in eighteen 1992 playoff games led the Blackhawks to the Stanley Cup Final for the first time since 1973.

Roenick repeated his 107-point '92-93 season in 1993-94, posting career highs with 61 assists and 125 penalty minutes. But as he entered the postseason with broken ribs and Chicago fell in the opening round of the playoffs for the second year in a row, a cloud seemed to pass over Roenick's career.

His contract remained unsettled, and he became the subject of trade rumors. Never one to edit himself, Roenick was openly critical of then-coach Darryl Sutter's conservative system, and during the labor dispute of 1994-95, Roenick was one of the players' union's most outspoken critics of management. He was not in game shape

I f I could play every game with blood on my face, I'd do it. It's just a mentality, a badge of honor.

when the season suddenly began, and his numbers showed it; just as his game was coming around, he collided with Dallas defenseman Derian Hatcher and suffered a knee bruise so severe it was thought he had torn ligaments and would be out until the middle of the following year. He forced himself back into action during the playoffs but was ineffective, and he himself became the focus of questions and criticism.

Tony Amonte, Roenick's teammate at Thayer and now in Chicago, would have none of it. "He loves to play hockey," Amonte says. "It's that simple. If one guy is going to play hurt, it's him. If he can walk, he's going to lace up his skates and go out there. That's why the stuff about him not willing to play really bothered him. If JR says he's hurt, you know he's hurt."

"Some of the comments he made got under the skin of some guys," says Blackhawks defenseman Steve Smith. "We all know that with what was said, right or wrong, Jeremy Roenick is a big-hearted kid who wants to win as much as any of us. . . . When the puck is dropped, that's the measure of a hockey player. And when the puck is dropped here, Jeremy Roenick is a pretty damn good hockey player."

"My only goal," affirms Roenick, "is to win a Stanley Cup with the Chicago Blackhawks."

Let's leave the last word to longtime Blackhawks broadcaster Pat Foley. "Jeremy's the first Blackhawk since Bobby [Hull] who combines the talent with the personality and the desire to be among the public," he says. "We don't like pretty boys in Chicago. We like this kid who will skate off the ice with his nose hanging by his ear and say, 'This is great!'"

*M\*A\*S\*H-Chicago's Jeremy Roenick meets New York's Jeff Beukeboom along the boards in front of the Blackhawks' bench.*

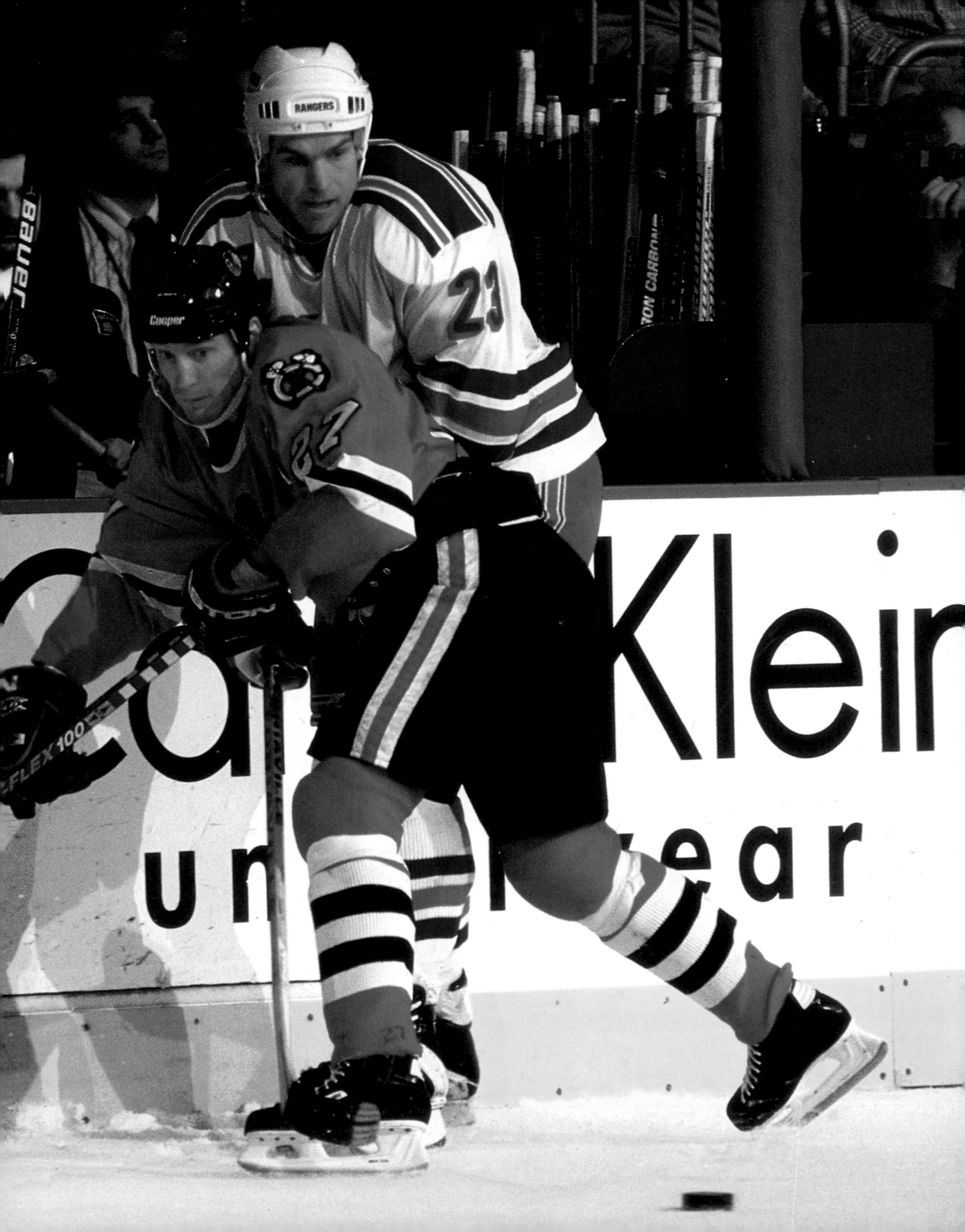
RANGERS
Cooper
23
Klein

# John Vanbiesbrouck

IT ISN'T OFTEN THAT A TEAM CAN LOSE THE FOURTH GAME OF A PLAYOFF SWEEP IN ITS OWN RINK—AND be treated to a raucous standing ovation by the hometown fans. Yet that is exactly what happened at the Miami Arena moments after Game 4 of the 1996 Stanley Cup Final. Even though the Florida Panthers had just been swept by the Colorado Avalanche, the Panthers' fans cheered loud and long for their plucky team. And the player for whom they cheered the loudest was their goalie, John Vanbiesbrouck. ⬤ Through the three short, amazing years of the Panthers' existence, the man they call Beezer had been the rock on which the franchise was built, and that was just as true for the club's Cinderella playoff run—and even for this Game 4, which had gone into a third overtime before Vanbiesbrouck and the Panthers finally succumbed, 1-0. "Beezer! Beezer!" chanted the fans, raining hundreds of their trademark plastic rats onto the ice in loving tribute. ⬤ "I stand here very disappointed, but very proud," he said after congratulating the Avalanche in the traditional handshake line. "This is something that I'll always remember. It was an epic game. I'm exhausted, I'm disappointed, but—in the same breath—I'm proud of our accomplishments." ⬤ Vanbiesbrouck reserved special praise for Avalanche goalie Patrick Roy, who had already won Stanley Cups in '86 and '93 with Montreal, becoming a French Canadian idol and the national team's netminder in the process. But Roy demanded a trade from the Habs during a midseason Forum blowout and was dealt to Colorado, where he became the last, crucial piece in the Avs' puzzle. In the Cup Final, although both had been magnificent, the butterfly specialist Roy had actually outplayed the small, darting Vanbiesbrouck—in the 104 minutes of Game 4, Roy turned aside all 63 shots he faced, Vanbiesbrouck 55 of 56, many seemingly impossible to stop—and Beezer, to no one's surprise, was man enough to admit it. "The performance that he had puts him up there with the greatest goalies of all time," he said of Roy. "I'm not afraid to say that." ⬤ And far too modest to admit to his own excellence. For the whole postseason, the 5-8 Detroit native kicked out an astonishing 685 of 735 shots, good for a jaw-dropping .932 save percentage. Measuring back from the '95-96 campaign, Vanbiesbrouck logged regular-season save percentages of .904, .914, and .924 in the three years of the fledgling Panthers' existence. When volume of shots faced is entered into the equation, Buffalo's great Czech netminder Dominik Hasek is the only NHL backstop of the mid-'90s with better numbers than the Beez. ⬤ Vanbiesbrouck's first 10 pro seasons were spent with the New York Rangers. His NHL debut, ironically, was a 1981 game in which he stopped 29 of 30 to beat the old Colorado Rockies in Denver's McNichols Arena. Back then he was always very consistent, very solid—a second-team junior league all-star, an MVP in the Central Hockey League, even a surprise winner of the Vezina Trophy in '85-86—but never truly among the game's elite.

But if the diminutive young goalie was not quite great, he certainly showed poise—something he had to have plenty of to survive on the mediocre Rangers of the '80s. That quality earned him the honor of becoming Team USA's regular goalkeeper, first at the '82 and '83 World Junior Championships, then at the '85, '87, '89, and '91 World Championships, as well as at the showcase tournament of the era, the '84, '87, and '91 Canada Cups.

However, 1989-90 marked the beginning of John Vanbiesbrouck's emergence from very good to among the very best. That season, rookie Mike Richter joined the Rangers and was installed as Vanbiesbrouck's co-starter. With the two Americans challenging each other to raise their game ever higher, the Broadway Blues soon found themselves in possession of the best net-minding tandem in the league.

Soon the vastly improved Rangers seemed close to the elusive Stanley Cup. But expansion loomed in the summer of 1993, and the club, forced to leave one of their goalies unprotected, chose to keep the younger one. Vanbiesbrouck eventually went to Florida (via Vancouver), shone in leading the first-year Panthers to within a single point of a playoff spot, and earned honors as a Second Team All-Star—yet had to feel a twinge of

We had 40 shots, we had our chances, but the guy in the net, you couldn't get a pea by him.

anguish as Richter and the Rangers won the Cup at last. Beezer sparkled again the following year, but again the neophyte club fell a thin point short of a postseason berth.

In the Panthers' third season, the Year of the Rat, everything came together—beginning on opening night when Scott Mellanby famously one-timed a scurrying rodent from the Panther dressing room to the Great Beyond. The team wound up the season finishing a strong fourth in the Eastern Conference. Vanbiesbrouck did have a rocky stretch—at one point he was pulled from the nets five separate times over a 14-game span. But he overcame the problems, thanks to the counseling of a sports psychologist and to a new commitment to religion, which, he said, were "giving me a feeling of calm like I've never had before."

At playoff time, first Boston, then Cup favorite Philadelphia fell before the Panthers' inspired checking, timely goal-scoring, and, most of all, Beezer's puck-stopping. "People say goalies can't win series by themselves these days," marveled Florida captain Brian Skrudland, "but, boy, if the Flyers series isn't proof of that, I don't know what is."

Then the Rat Pack rallied to oust Lemieux, Jagr, and the rest of the Pittsburgh Penguins' Flying Circus, Vanbiesbrouck capping the upset with a 39-saves-in-40-shots Game 7 performance at the Civic Arena. "We wouldn't have won if it wasn't for Beezer," said Panther Tom Fitzgerald. Said a rueful Pens coach Eddie Johnston: "We had 40 shots, we had our chances, but the guy in net, you couldn't get a pea by him."

That set the stage for the '96 Cup Final. It was

not a close series—the Avalanche were simply too strong, and Florida had finally run out of miracles—but it was aptly emblematic of the new NHL. The Panthers were a new club, playing in as unhockey a place as could be: yet the fans of South Florida went absolutely wild for their team and for the game. The Avs were even newer, having moved at the start of the season from the hockey bastion of Quebec; but the Denver fans went wild too, and were mindful enough of the game's past to hold up "Thank You, Quebec" signs during the Cup run.

The Avalanche's roster distilled the game's new worldliness. There were plenty of French Canadians, holdovers from the days of the Nordiques, along with two new additions: Roy and nonpareil aggravator Claude Lemieux. The most artistic skater of all was Joe Sakic, an English Canadian—unless it was Valeri

Kamensky, a Russian. The toughest two-way player was Peter Forsberg, a Swede, whose grit was augmented by linemate Scott Young, an American. The top attacking defenseman was Sandis Ozolinsh, a Latvian; and the team's steadiest blueliner, as well as the scorer of the Cup-winning goal in the third overtime, was Uwe Krupp, a German.

The Beezer, heroic as he'd been, was simply overwhelmed by this Avalanche from the summits of hockey's brave new world. But he'd still done himself proud.

"There wasn't much to say," Vanbiesbrouck recalled after encountering Roy on the traditional handshake line. "He was anxious to grab the Cup, and I was anxious to get out of there. All I could say was, 'Congratulations, you deserved it.'" True enough, but in fact, they both deserved it.

*LEAVE IT TO BEEZER- When Florida's defense falters, goaltender John Vanbiesbrouck often comes up with the big save.*

## AUTHORS' NOTE

The World Cup and the 1996-1997 NHL season are nearly upon us, leaving us barely a moment in which to thank the multitude of people who make the book you're holding possible: Charlie Schmitt, NHL Director of Publishing, who conceived the project and shaped it in its initial stages; our superb agent, David Vigliano, who got us on board and kept a vigilant eye throughout; Elle Farrell at the NHL, who saw the project through its latter stages and handled the photo captions in the tension-filled final seconds of play; and the many people who assisted our research, particularly Nexus wizard Denise Kiernan, as well as interviewer Terry Lefton and the many fine folks in NHL team publicity departments, notably Chris Brown in Hartford, Barbara Davidson in Chicago,

Barry Hanrahan in Tampa Bay, Rusty Ingram in Boston, Bill Jamieson and Tony Lasher in Detroit, Tracey Olsen in Colorado, Dominick Saillant and Vivianne Slade in Ottawa, Casey Vanden Heuvel in Toronto, and Bruce Wawrzyniak in Buffalo. Special gratitude for their extraordinary patience and professionalism is owed to Walton Rawls and Jim Davis at Turner Publishing. Thanks as always to our families and close friends for their enthusiasm and moral support; and finally, the authors, once again, thank each other.

JEFF Z. KLEIN, New York
KARL-ERIC REIF, Buffalo

## NHL ACKNOWLEDGMENTS

Arthur Pincus
Bernadette Mansur
Mary Pat Clarke
Greg Inglis
Photo captions by Tamir Lipton and Adam Schwartz.

Rick Dudley
Richard Zahnd
Ed Horne
Charlie Schmitt
Elle Farrell
Mary Trapani
Doug Perlman
Ruth Gruhin

## PHOTO CREDITS

### Allsport USA
pp. 4-5, Al Bello; p. 14, Glenn Cratty; p. 16, Glenn Cratty; p. 18, Glenn Cratty; p. 20, Al Bello; p. 22, Tim Defrisco; p. 30, Glenn Cratty; p. 58, Tim Defrisco; p. 60, Rick Stewart; p. 62, Glenn Cratty; p. 70, Glenn Cratty, p. 82, J. D. Cuban; p. 115, Rick Stewart; p. 122, C. J. Relke; p. 124, Glenn Cratty; p. 129, Robert Laberge; p. 138-9, Al Bello; p. 144, Jamie Squire; pp. 148-9, Glenn Cratty

Scott Levy; p. 100, J. Giamundo; p. 102, B. Wippert; p. 106, Bruce Bennett; p. 108, J. Leary; pp. 110-1, Bruce Bennett; p. 112, C. Anderson; p. 116, M. Hicks; p. 119, Bruce Bennett; p. 130, J. Leary; p. 136, J. Giamundo; p. 140, Bruce Bennett; p. 146, J. Leary; p. 150, A. Foxall; p. 152, Bruce Bennett; p. 154-5, Bruce Bennett; p. 156, Brian Winkler; p. 159, J. Giamundo

### Bruce Bennett Studios
p. 10, Bruce Bennett; p. 12, Bruce Bennett; p. 24, Bruce Bennett; p. 33, Bruce Bennett; p. 34, J. Giamundo; p. 37, J. Giamundo; p. 38, J. Giamundo; p. 40, Bruce Bennett; p. 42, Scott Levy; p. 44, R. Laberge; p. 48, Bruce Bennett; p. 51, Bruce Bennett; pp. 52-3, Len Redkoles; p. 54, J. McIsaacs; p. 65, Bruce Bennett; p. 74, M. Hicks; p. 76, Bruce Bennett Studios; pp. 78-9, J. Giamundo; p. 80, A. Foxall; p. 84, Bruce Bennett; p. 87, Bruce Bennett; p. 88, Bruce Bennett; p. 90, Bruce Bennett; p. 94, C. Anderson; p. 96, Bruce Bennett; p. 98,

### Mark Hill/TBS, Inc.
pp. 7-8, 46-7, 68-9, 92-3, 120-1

### Focus On Sports
pp. 26, 28, 56, 66-7, 73, 104, 134, 143

### Sports Photo Masters, Inc.
p. 126, Don Smith; p. 133, Craig Melvin

Front Cover: Bill Wippert